to dream the impossible dream

Wilda Sue Marple

Miss W. Virginia

Whitaker House

PITTSBURGH AND COLFAX STREETS, SPRINGDALE, PA. 15144

To Dream the Impossible Dream

Wilda Sue Marple
Route 2, Box 16-A
Rutherfordton, NC 28139

Quotations from *The Living Bible* © 1971, used by permission of Tyndale House, Wheaton, Illinois.

Excerpt from the song entitled *The Impossible Dream (The Quest)*, lyrics by Joe Darion, music by Mitch Leigh. Copyright © 1965 Andrew Scott, Inc. and Helena Music Corp. International copyright secured. Made in U.S.A. All rights reserved. Used by permission.

Contents

Foreword by Vicki Jamison

I had no idea that I would become as involved in a book as I became with this one. I felt I was living my life in many areas that were very similar to Wilda Sue.

This story will inspire you and cause faith to rise in your heart. I know that with God all things indeed are possible.

To my mother and father, who instilled in me the vision to see, the faith to believe, and the courage to do.

To my husband, Bill, who is my other half, and together we are one. Without the cooperation and sacrifice of Bill and the children, this book could never have been written.

Chapter One

The Impossible Dream

Spotlights...glittering smiles...the brass-spangled fanfare...

Royal purple carpet unfolds slowly as the room swells with an expectant hush. It's the Fashion Two-Twenty "Royal Road to Riches"—the grand finale of the world-wide awards ceremony held each year.

And like so many times before, Bill and I sit waiting for the suspense-filled moment when the crescendo builds and the number one distributor in the world is announced to thundering applause.

It's more like the Academy Awards than a business convention. Spotlights bathe the thousands in swirling wisps.

We sit figeting—will we be tops in the world again? Will we—like we have year after year since 1976—once again walk down the purple runway searching past the spotlights for familiar faces?

It's been an incredible career in the cosmetic world. Our retail dollar figure has risen far beyond our wildest dreams. It's been a lot of work (how little the people know!), but it's also been quite rewarding—no one can know the feeling of being "on top of it all" unless he or she has been there.

My thoughts are suddenly drawn back to the grand moment—I hear "Bill and Wilda Sue Marple" announced! My chest is pounding and my stomach fluttering. I look through tear-brimmed eyes at the thousands of applauding business people. As the band breaks into "The Impossible Dream," Fashion Two-Twenty's theme song, a million thoughts rush through my mind. I can't help thinking that my place in the spotlight could easily have been filled by someone else.

So many times the dream was almost snuffed out and killed.

I wonder what the people would think if they knew the real me. They see me dressed in a beautiful long gown and sparkling diamonds—but what if they could see past my spotlit smile and glittering clothes?

If only all those people knew the *real* story—the bittersweet days in the West Virginia "holler" shack as the ragamuffin daughter of a penniless drunk...the moments of grandeur as a beauty queen and would-be Hollywood starlet...the pregnant and almost-barefoot days out trying to ignite my dream in the cosmetic business...and the bottomless pit that I had stumbled into even as I rose to the top of the business world.

If only they had been there to see what drove me on—that emptiness, that vacuum. If only they knew the extremes I had gone to in search of fulfillment.

And if only they could see how that search has led me to the greatest fulfillment anyone could ever know.

If only they knew that they can make it, too... that the dream is merely beginning.

Chapter Two

Once Upon A Dream

It was almost like a scene out of Loretta Lynn's *Coal Miner's Daughter.* Mother was only twelve years old when she met the man who would be my father. He was twenty. For him, it was more than mere friendship. Years later he would say, "She was the prettiest little girl I ever saw."

As she matured, Daddy's first thoughts proved true and long-lasting. My mother, Garnett Hayes, was voted the "Prettiest Girl" in her high school. She was from a staunch Baptist background, and it was her great desire to someday serve on a mission field. That was her utmost longing as a child and young girl—to travel and take the Gospel to some remote area of the world. It was a dream my mother held in her heart for years.

Daddy, Raymond Lee Estep, was the fartherest possible thing from a missionary. He was a handsome and happy-go-lucky, guitar-pickin', fun-lovin' man. He kept finding excuses to come over to Mother's house—mainly to bring the guitar and sing love songs. Everyone knew him as the handsome boy with the big, wide smile.

Maybe it was the love songs, maybe the little black curl that always fell down on his forehead when he sang to her, or perhaps that boyish grin—whatever it was, it worked. By the time she was sixteen, she had fallen "head over heels" in love with him. They were married that next year—Christmas Eve, 1938. She was seventeen; he was twenty-five.

When Mother and Daddy were first married, he built a little cabin in Jordan Creek. Carol was their first-born. Then I came.

By the time I was old enough to start remembering things, we had moved to Young's Bottom and were living in a basement apartment below a general store. My brother, Jerry, and two younger sisters, Joyce and Ellen, were born while we lived in Young's Bottom.

Another family lived in the store basement, also. One of the few things that I recollect from that dingy place was the other family's mother reaching through the separating window to hand us cookies. It's interesting what our little minds pick up—and interesting what we choose to forget.

One experience that really stands out in my mind was the time it rained so hard that the water rolled off the hillsides above the general store, through the cracks, and flooded the basement where we lived. Mother was pregnant with Ellen, but she kept scurring about as the water seeped in—first moving the furniture, then stacking the furniture up as the dirty water swirled around the room, all the while dipping water out with a bucket. We had so few things anyway, which made the water damage even worse—so many things were totally ruined, including what few pictures she had.

Survival seems to be the only word for those times. We certainly weren't happy. It was a "hand-to-mouth" existence—and often with empty hands! We were dirt poor. It was nothing unusual for us to go to bed with a wrenching, hungry feeling, often cold as well. We lived little better than primitive generations before us had lived in the "hollers"—the valleys snuggled in the hills of West Virginia.

All of us kids were starved for affection, kind of like orphan kittens. My first emotions were of fear, loneliness, and hunger. Child psychologists say that most of a person's personality is set during those first several years—I guess that's so. I always longed to be loved.

When my baby sister, Ellen, was born, Mother had gone to the hospital to have the baby. I was so glad to see her when she returned that I started to get up on the bed where she was lying, but she said, "No! Wilda, you might hurt the baby!" I didn't know what was happening. I didn't know the word "rejection," but I knew the ache in my heart. It was so hard for a little child like myself to understand why a little pink bundle would make my mother so jumpy. I just knew that I felt so alone and unloved.

It must have been difficult for my mother, but I only knew that she didn't have time to pull me up on her lap much anymore or rock and hold me.

Mother went to work shortly after Ellen was born. She took a scrub-woman's job at the Daniel Boone Hotel in Charleston, working the midnight shift.

I was so lonely for her. I guess lots of children experience this feeling sometimes, but it seemed that my mother was never home to quench that aching feeling inside me. As we children grew, we learned how to lean on each other—five little pups hovering together and comforting each other. Carol—even as a little girl—became a substitute mother to us. She took Joyce as her "baby" and I took Ellen—we helped care for them. And—of course—Jerry was sandwiched between all of us—we all tried to take care of him.

I was the second in line, eighteen months younger than Carol.

Jerry was just twenty months younger than me. He was the gentle, humble child—the wood-carryer, the yodeler, the marble-shooter, and the "pride and joy" of all us girls. How he survived being the only boy in a family with four girls—I will never know!

Joyce was next in line, two years younger than Jerry. She had snow-white hair and sky-blue eyes. She was frail and moved around very slowly (we called her "slow-poke"), yet she was venturesome,

13

too. More than once she fell out of a tree or got hurt in some other precarious way—the time she fell out of a tree and played "dead" scared several years out of all us children! Yet she was always so interested in others, always took up for the underdog in any situation.

Ellen, the baby, was thirteen months younger than Joyce. She was very quiet, sorta stand-offish, crying when strangers came around. But as she grew she had a compassionate heart—always seeing other people who had it hard, too.

Hard—everything was hard on Mother. It was such a different world from the one she had grown up in. Although her parents weren't extremely rich, they had been able to live well. She had grown up in a nice, Christian home with a lot of security and respect. But the world she was thrust into as a bride and mother was just the opposite. A woman who lived close to us practiced witchcraft. For whatever reason, she invoked some kind of a curse on Mother and all of us children. It filled my mother's heart with fear. Then, one of the neighbors gave Mother a "way" to break the curse—"Cut a piece of hair from each of the kids' heads and burn the hairs!" Mother did the strange ritual, but still she lived in fear that the curse would bring sudden harm to her or her brood.

But for mother, our living conditions and the backwoods voodoo were small problems in comparison to another—her husband. When they were dating, he was the romantic, the singer, her protector. Soon after marriage, however, all of that began—bit by bit—to change.

She soon found out just how much she had "bitten off." She loved to go to church; he liked to pal around with his drinkin' buddies.

By the time she was twenty-four, she had already given birth to five little children—all before the first-born reached six years old.

It was the first years of the Second World War—the bleak, miserable years as Americans faced scarcity with food coupons and rations, and that Madman across the water kept threatening to turn the world into a Nazi nightmare.

Then, after the war, Daddy was laid off from his job with United States Rubber Company, and that's when she had to go out and look for a job...any job.

At twenty-five, Mother's dreams of love and marriage were erased by the hard, hungry years. Her love-song singin', smiling man had become a hardened, self-centered husband. Life had turned out so horribly different than the dreams of a starry-eyed teenager.

Chapter Three

Don't Come Home A' Drinkin'

My father came home very little. He worked as a brick-layer and carpenter during the warm months, but only as the weather would allow. Even then, many nights and weekends he would be out with his buddies, "feeling his cheerios," as Mother used to call it.

When he would come home on a binge, he would do almost anything to torment us and pick a fight. He would be surly and mean—especially to Mother.

When he would get this way, Mother knew that it could go on for awhile. She would take it as long as she could, then finally take all five of us from home and run for fear he would hurt her or the children.

Home by this time (I was five years old) was a piece of land up in Mill Holler on Jordan's Creek— not far from where my parents had lived when they first married. It was two miles from the main road. Needless to say, we had to walk everywhere we went—including when we left my father.

I remember all of us running several times to a neighboring farm and sleeping the rest of the night under a big tree with the neighbor's cows moving around us. In a strange way, it was comforting just knowing that the cows were there and that we weren't all alone.

Other times we would go to Mother's parents. Each time, Daddy would finally come and get us. When he was off the booze, he was the most gentle-manly, apologetic man in the world. He would always promise never to get drunk and be mean again.

But he always did. Everytime he did, the same gripping, horrifying fear filled our hearts. No one can fully describe the dread that was forever etched on our little minds. It was a dread born from many harrowing experiences.

There was a time when Mother waited for Daddy to go get something more to drink, then she went to the nearest phone a mile or so away to ask her father to come get all of us.

Grandpa drove to the foot of the holler, and we walked down to meet him. It had been raining for several days so there was a lot of "backwater"— when the river becomes so swollen that it backs up to the creek. We had to cross one extremely bad backwater. Mother went first across the fragile little footbridge; each of us came behind holding on to one another's hands, cringing across the timbers until we made it safely to the other side. The night air was singed with dread that Daddy would catch us leaving and make us go back home. So on we went, following Mother, one pudgy little hand gripping the next...all of us wet and frozen with terror. I remember that particular night, not just because of the fear-filled walk down to the waiting car, but because I got so excited to be riding in Grandpa's car, and so happy to be with Grandma and Grandpa, that I opened my door as we drove into their garage and the car door was literally torn off! Mother tried to whip me, but her sister, Aunt Opal, wouldn't let her. By this time, we were all numb from the fearful dread and inner-sickness.

But once again, Daddy came for us after he sobered. And once again he got Mother to listen to his pleas, so we all went back home.

Not long after this, our hard life proved too much for Mother—all the strain and disillusionment. Her good health was gone. She ended up in the hospital with exhaustion. During her stay, she had to have a hysterectomy.

During this time, Daddy hired a babysitter for us, at least that's what we were told. It became evident that the babysitter was more for Daddy's benefit than ours. Soon he started pickin' the guitar and singing love songs to her.

I'll never forget the day Mother came home from the hospital. Her parents brought her—she was in a full-length, blue housecoat. We swarmed around her with hot-flowing tears pouring down our faces—five little kids with so much love for our mother.

But it was only a night or so later that we were suddenly awakened by that familiar, dreaded noise—our parents were fighting. Finally, we heard Daddy yell, "Get out of the house! *Get out of the house!*"

It was pitch-dark and pouring down rain, but we heard him force Mother to leave. I could only lie in bed, trembling through the night, wondering where my dear mama was.

The next day we found that she was so weak that she knew she could never make it to the highway. So she spent the night under a rock cliff nearby—trying to survive the rain-soaked night. She only had that blue housecoat over her frail little ninety-eight pound body.

The next day, after she had rested awhile, she managed to walk to the highway to the nearest phone and call her parents. They told her to, "Wait right there!"

In the meantime, we children had been led to the chicken house by the babysitter and locked inside. We didn't know what was going on, so we comforted each other and settled down, waiting to be let out. Every once in a while, we would peer through the cracks in the chicken house hoping to catch a glimpse of the babysitter coming to let us out.

After some time, we finally saw our grandparents and Mother trudging up the hill. I can still recall the terror, shivering as I stood with my sisters and brother, looking through the cracks...not knowing what would happen to my little mother walking slowly behind her parents toward what had become a horror-filled house.

Like an echo exploding throughout the holler, I heard my daddy yell. Then I saw him stick a long-barreled shotgun out through the attic window. I was too young to know just how tense the situation was, but I knew that one way or the other Grandma and Grandpa would protect my mother.

Harsh words were screamed back and forth. Daddy was trying to get them to turn around and go back—"Get outta here or I'm gonna fill you full of bullets!"

If my grandmother was scared, she didn't show it—all eighty-nine pounds of her rose up as she hollered back—"They *eat* bullets where I come from!"

I've blocked out the rest of the day from my memory—all the words and threats. All I remember is that eventually they got my dad calmed down long enough to talk. By day's end, we were back in the house—all relatively safe and sound. Soon afterwards, the live-in babysitter was forced to leave. For a time, we had Mother at home and Daddy acting right, but soon...

Mother got well enough to go back to work, and we had to go back to shifting for ourselves. Life was hard and coarse. There was little room for dreams...only cold survival. Most survived life in the holler, but dreams almost always died, killed by the elements, the poverty, and the bitter struggles.

Chapter Four

A Different Daddy

Daddy was a curious mix of kindness and hatred, meekness and meanness. When the booze wore off, he would beg, "Garnett, oh, Garnett—I love you...I'll never touch another drop." When he was off the liquor, he would sing and play the guitar with us children for hours.

But that same man—because of his volatile temper (especially when the temper was mixed with liquor)—could become an entirely different person. He would become a father who could, for example, force his little girl, Joyce, to throw a sick "biddie" (newborn chick) on a rock to "kill it and put it outta its misery."

With his upbringing, Daddy should have been different. His mother was from a Methodist background—a staunch believer. She went through very rough years with her eleven children, especially after her husband (Daddy's father) was run over by a truck in November one year. Daddy spoke more than once about that sad Thanksgiving.

Before he was killed, my grandfather had bought a fifty-acre tract of land up at the head of the Lind's Fork Holler by trading one cow for the land—it was during the Great Depression and immediate food must have been more valuable than rocky ground! On the land, Daddy's parents had built a five-room house in the shape of an "L" with an attached porch all the way around. They also added a barn, corn crib, smokehouse, and cellar.

Daddy's mother had lived on this farm all through the Depression and war years, bringing up eleven children and working.

But in late 1945, when I was six years old, she sent for all her children. She wanted to see all eleven of them before she died. It crushed my daddy to see her nearing the end. As she lay there, she asked Daddy if he knew the Lord as his "personal Savior." Just minutes before she died—as my daddy sat by her bedside—she put her hands up to her "little Raymond" and asked him if he would "accept Jesus." He slowly replied, "Yes, Mama, some-day..."

Then, she was gone.

In his own way, my daddy idolized his mother. He felt a tremendous sense of guilt for the way he had treated her as a teenager. So when she passed away, an era ended for him. All of her words finally started to "hit home."

After Grandmother died, Daddy's brothers and sisters asked him to go live on the old homeplace. They didn't want the house to "go down," and it seemed that he was the most likely choice to take over the farm.

So one day not long after Grandmother's burial, Daddy and his buddy pulled up to our Mill Holler home with a borrowed truck, loaded our few belongings, and took us to our "new" home. That home was located two miles up Lind's Fork Holler, one mile past the end of a passable road. We drove as far as the road went, then had some young boys who lived in the holler use their horse and wagon to take the furniture and clothing that last mile over a path.

A whole new life began for us—in more ways than one. To five, little, "poor" kids, the Lind's Fork cabin was beautiful, though by today's standards here in America, it would be totally unfit for anyone.

Summers were warm and fun-filled, especially after Jerry made a little dam of stones and backed the creek up enough for us to have a genuine swimmin' hole.

The winters were fierce in comparison. Often we would have to walk the two miles to the school bus through several feet of snow. Even at night, with the fireplace glowing from red-hot embers, it was always so very cold. If there's one thing I can painfully recall from my childhood—next to my daddy's erratic behavior—it's the all-winter feeling of never getting unchilled.

Before we moved to the head of Lind's Fork

24

Holler, life had been an unending hell for Mother, for us children, and even for Daddy. I didn't understand then how he was bitterly torn between his need for the bottle and his love for us. There must have been a tremendous sense of guilt involved, but no amount of begging for forgiveness or good intentions seemed to change his ways. The only antidote for his own lack of love and feelings of inadequacy seemed to be the never-ending, guilt-quencher—the bottle.

He had been that way for more than a decade, and it was the general consensus that his thirst for the bottle would no doubt break up his home for good and drive him even deeper into the liquid trap he had fallen into. That's the way it always seemed to work. Once a drunk, always a hopeless drunk.

But my mother never gave up on him. I'm sure that she wanted to. I'm equally sure that most of her friends and relatives thought that she was senseless, subjecting herself and her children to a futile, cruel fate by giving in again and again to his "please come home" apologies.

But Mother didn't give up praying for Daddy—no matter how horribly he treated her. And when we moved to Lind's Fork, she began to see some prayer-answers unfolding, however slowly.

Maybe it was the fact that Daddy was much farther away from the destructive influence of his old drinkin' buddies.

Maybe it was the reminders of Daddy's praying mother as he looked around the Lind's Fork house—the red roses rambling over the rock cliffs, the childhood memories of kind words and bittersweet regrets.

Or could it have been the death-bed promise that he had uttered to his mother when she asked him to accept Jesus as his Lord and Savior? Did he remember his words to her, "I will...someday"?

Perhaps it was my mother's undying faithfulness—even when she had plenty of reasons not to stand by her man.

Whatever it was—my daddy reached a turning point in his life, a change that finally helped him make an eternal decision.

One night—not too long after we moved to Lind's Fork—my daddy's brother and sister-in-law, Uncle Dallas and Aunt Delcey, came and took Mother and Daddy to church with them.

My old daddy never came back! In his place, a new man came home—a man who had gone to Lucey Wilson Baptist Church merely to appease his wife and brother, but at the end of the service, he had walked down the aisle and poured out his guilts and shortcomings on an old rustic altar.

Moments later, as he begged outloud for forgiveness, God spoke audibly to him—"You don't have to continue begging. The price has already been paid. You are forgiven."

We were asleep when Daddy and Mother

walked down that old familiar path to the house. The next morning I awoke to hear them talking softly.

That same daddy—the one who had shown up for dates with my mother long ago with a slimy, black snake wrapped around his neck, and the man who had shot a hole through his mother's Bible— this man was now talking softly and using words like "salvation" and "sanctification."

My daddy stumbled several times after that; he even "hit the bottle" a few times. But each time he did, he was the most miserable man alive. He just didn't have the taste for it anymore. He was a changed man, each time repenting of his shortcomings.

Mother's dream for a Christian home had almost died. It could easily have been snuffed out like an ember drenched with rainwater. Everyone called my mother's dream totally impossible— everyone except Mother.

Chapter Five

Developing Dreams

I can remember often after that special night, I would wake up during the twilight hours and hear my parents talking softly. To many children those soft murmurs would have meant little, but to one who had spent almost nine years waking up to vile, harsh words, those night-time conversations between my parents were like fresh lullabies. God had already begun restoring all those years of pain for our family.

Daddy began writing songs again. One of the greatest changes was that he had time to start developing us children into a singing group. After teaching us "parts," Daddy got us interested in learning to play instruments. Before long, Carol had learned to play the mandolin and guitar, I had learned the Spanish guitar, and Jerry eventually mastered both the steel and Spanish guitars. Ellen later developed into a good guitar player, while Joyce mainly concentrated on singing.

Daddy worked with us, and even gave us a

name, the Starlight Quartet. We used to alternate between Joyce and Ellen because they were both so young at the time. (Today, my sister, Ellen, and her family are still performing under the name Starlight Singers.)

As children, we didn't know how good we were until we started appearing in a few area churches. I don't think we meant it to develop like it did, but before long we were traveling quite a bit in Uncle Dallas' pick-up truck—all dressed alike in pretty clothes Aunt Delcey and Mother had made for us.

As our singing became more professional, every Sunday we would get dressed and walk the two miles to the main highway to catch the Greyhound bus. We rode with Daddy to Charleston to meet Mother (she worked all night), then we would sing on WTIP and WCHS radio stations before making the return trip home together.

We sang all over the area, and eventually were good enough to do the Ted Mack "Amateur Hour" the time it was broadcast from Channel 3 in Huntington, West Virginia.

We especially thought it was great when Daddy went to Charleston and bought a brand new record player/recorder that came complete with blank records. He made records of us singing and gave them to friends and relatives. To kids of the next generation, those first recording/playback sessions would seem "small potatoes" compared with the easy-to-buy cassette tapings. But to five little kids with nothing but songs and grins, it was the ultimate!

The people that we sang to were about as poor as we were, so we didn't make much from the church offerings, but to us it became a very serious thing. If someone could have had the time, energy, money, and know-how to "package" us—who knows?

I loved that special feeling of my soaring spirit as I "made" music, and I believe that it was the beginning of yet another dream to add to my growing collection.

Singing was one release from an otherwise destitute world. Even after my daddy changed so drastically, many things did not change. We were still desperately poor, though my parents were working as much as possible.

As I grew up, I heard others say that they were poor when they were young, but they didn't know it. Well, I knew it; nothing—my home, my school, the holler—would let me forget it. How I hated being different and poor.

The majority of people in the holler were related in one way or the other—except for us, so we were oddballs even in that.

School was anything but wonderful. I loved the learning part of it, but from the first day that this little, knobby-kneed girl stood waiting for the big yellow school bus, I always knew that I was different. The other kids were not well-off, by any means, but at least they had enough to buy a few nice clothes and special things.

The comparisons were always there. My brother and sisters and I brought sack lunches of pinto-bean sandwiches or potatoes 'n onions. Other kids either bought school lunches or had "delicacies" like peanut butter or lunch meat. To others on the "inside," it meant nothing, but to me—especially as my little schoolgirl mind blew it out of proportion—it was the ever-present cloud separating me from the rest of my classmates.

One lunch I'll never forget. I brought a green bean sandwich. One of the little girls asked me, "What is *that*?" When I told her, she ran away for a moment, then returned with one of her little friends. Each laugh and taunt were like stabs with a rusty knife right into my heart. Would the wounds ever heal?

The most poignant incident of all was the Easter during my first grade. Our class had planned a big Easter egg hunt. All of the first grade pupils were to bring their own Easter eggs so that we could leave school early and go over to the big grassy farm near the school—the farm owned by the fourth grade teacher's father. My fears heightened as the time arrived for us to go from the school to the farm that day. I had to go, but I knew that soon everyone would know my "secret."

My mother didn't have any eggs and couldn't

spare the money needed to buy them, so I couldn't take any pretty eggs to the hunt.

I stood that day and watched as the other children kept piling those beautiful eggs together. It would have been the most wondrous sight—all those multicolored eggs heaped together, but I couldn't see past the hot, brimming tears that I kept trying to wipe away.

I felt that I couldn't join in the fun since I didn't bring anything to contribute. So, instead of at least trying to act happy and excited, I withdrew into a shell and acted like it didn't bother me.

With the pit of my stomach flaming, I went over to the highway and stood counting the passing cars.

"One...two..."

No one seemed to notice me. The teachers had hidden the eggs by then and all the other children were scurrying around collecting them from behind bushes and grassy nests.

"three...four...five..."

If they *had* seen me or had gotten my attention, I wanted them to know that I was having fun *all by myself*.

"...six...seven..."

I kept counting as far as my first grade education would allow, then started naming the different kinds of cars, "Chevy...Packard,..." thinking of all the other times when I had been "different," like the times when all the other children would line up with nickels clasped in hand, waiting for the occasional cookie and orange juice treat.

That Easter egg hunt was only one of many other times when I would feel separated and different. But that afternoon as I stood counting cars by the side of the road—it marked the beginning of another dream—an agonizing, searing search. I knew above anything else that I wanted to *be somebody* and have lots of money when I grew up. I thought that if I had plenty of money, I could then buy the things I wanted, and that would surely make me happy and accepted.

It seemed impossible, but the dream was already firmly implanted in my veins. Raging! Someway...somehow I would reach the place where I wouldn't have to stand on the outside looking in.

Even as a little West Virginia ragamuffin, I vowed with everything I had inside me to escape this bottomless pit called poverty.

Whatever it took, my dream *would* develop until I succeeded.

Chapter Six

The Dreams Grow

The next years were filled with adventures, especially after Daddy changed so drastically for the better. Money was still "scarce as hen's teeth," but at least the always-constant childhood terror was gone from home.

When I was twelve, I started "bloomin' out" as we called it in the hills. Not long after, Mother bought my first bra, what girl can forget that? I had become so embarrassed at being the only girl without one that I hated running (and bouncing) during recess. I tried to walk slump-shouldered to avoid the obvious. What a dream fulfilled!

It was about that same time that I overheard my mother and father talking one day about moving out of the holler. Daddy didn't want any of us kids marrying into any of the other holler families. Somehow he was able to make a deal—he bought a tract of land from my mother's grandmother. It was located in Walgrove, West Virginia.

Daddy built a little makeshift five-room house

for us to live in at Walgrove—a temporary place that would be our home for the next five years until he completed his "dream house," a nine-room home that even had running water and a bathroom inside! That temporary house in Walgrove (like the rest before that we had lived in) had a "path out back" for a toilet and no running water, except when one of us "ran" and got it! But it did have one light bulb hanging in every room and one gas stove to keep the entire house warm (we had to make a "beeline" every morning from the warm beds to huddle around the stove as we got dressed for school).

The cold often led to accidents. Many charred chimneys stand as eerie tombstones to mid-winter house-fires, but the most terror-filled accident was much more personal.

We were waiting at the bus stop. It was freezing cold with a few snowflakes filtering down from the gray sky. Some of the bigger boys had brought a bucket of "drip" gas (unrefined—from the holding tanks) to burn so that we could huddle around the can and stay somewhat warm during our wait for the bus.

Somehow, after the fire was started in the bucket, it was kicked over on my brother. In an instant, the liquid flames swarmed over little Jerry! He became a living torch. Someone ran for Daddy. A passing truck driver stopped, ran and grabbed Carol's coat, and knocked Jerry down into the snow—smothering the flames with the coat.

We saw that Jerry was in serious condition, and by the time Daddy ran down to the stop, Jerry was screaming uncontrollably. The sight—it still evokes a sickening feeling—of Daddy rolling up Jerry's pant legs and seeing the skin roll down on top of his socks—no one can forget that.

Jerry was rushed to the nearest hospital and treated. The days to come were filled with increasing agony. He had been given medicine and bandaged before being sent back home, but a week later Jerry was in such pain that Mother took him back to the doctor. When he took the bandages off, the flesh rolled off as well. Jerry was beginning to develop gangrene and a blood-red streak ran up to his hips. It was extremely serious—the fluid had leaked off of his knees.

As he sadly surveyed the damaged little body, the doctor shook his head and told my mother that her son would probably never walk again. Then he put Jerry in the hospital to get the infection under control. Finally, he was able to start grafting skin from other parts of Jerry's body onto his legs.

Mother was determined that Jerry would get well, and that he would walk again. She began praying for him, begging God to touch her only son. She had gone through so much through the years, but she knew that God would hear her prayers. She was determined. . .and faithful.

It wasn't overnight, but soon Jerry's legs began healing. He had to go through many painful skin grafts, but his legs continued to mend. Mother prayed for him day after day, even after he was released from the hospital. Before long, that little dark-haired boy with the sparkling eyes was tottering on two wobbly, stiff legs. The first steps were excruciating, but he was too young and too proud to languish in bed for the rest of his life. Soon he was walking with only a slight limp. Then he began begging Daddy to take him fishing in the river—he loved that more than anything. As time progressed, Jerry started to run and play. The doctors didn't understand how a hopelessly crippled little boy could be so healthy and spry. But Mother did.

Those teenage years were a special time for my dreams to develop.

Finally, when I was seventeen, the big house was finished—almost too late for me to enjoy it.

Moving into the big house was a brand new world for us. Instead of all of us kids being squeezed into two dingy little rooms, Carol and I had our own bedroom, Joyce and Ellen were in another bedroom, and Jerry had his own bedroom for the first time in his life (he was sixteen)—now that really seemed like luxury to us!

Also, about this same time, we got our first telephone. To a teenage girl, it was the "ultimate." I remember that first telephone mostly because of Blaine.

When I was fourteen, this wonderfully handsome guy worked through my Aunt Opal to get Daddy (who had always told us that we couldn't date until we reached our fifteenth birthday) to let me go to a Saturday afternoon matinee.

Before long, Blaine and I were "going steady." Everyone at school thought we were made for each other—they called him "Tony Curtis" and me "Jane Russel." Blaine and I became best friends as well as "steadies." He was my "first love" (who can forget that *first* love?), and it helped me grow in self-confidence and self-esteem. I was accepted and loved as I was.

But my dad saw us getting serious much too early during the next year or so (painful reminders to him of a not too distant past). He began letting me know about his displeasure.

Another problem came between Blaine and me. Blaine knew that I was religious—that we had been traveling Gospel singers as children—even though I didn't push it on him. But during my fifteenth year, as I sat in a little Baptist church near Walgrove, I felt the need to open my heart to Jesus Christ. In all those years, it had never been as plain to me as it was that night; I realized that Jesus Christ had been just a religious fact to me before, not a personal Savior.

So that night, in response to the pastor's invitation, I went down to the altar and accepted Jesus Christ into my heart. I had read and sung about Him for years, but nothing compared to that night when I asked Him to forgive me of my sins and give me the promise of eternal life.

I can't even begin to describe the excitement in my heart as God's love melted through my soul. I got up from the altar singing, "Oh, How I Love Jesus!"

After I had accepted Jesus at that altar, I wanted everyone else to know Him, too. I especially couldn't understand why Blaine was so noncommittal about something that brought me so much happiness and fulfillment.

The change really began for me at church. Someone at our church had made a poster and left it on the altar to write our prayer requests on. I wrote Blaine's mother and grandmother on that list. When Blaine saw it, he was highly offended.

That was the turning point of our relationship. Little things began to fit together—Blaine's jealousy, my Daddy's concern for both of us.

One Sunday morning, I picked up the *Parade Magazine* that comes with many Sunday newspapers. On the front cover was a photograph of Prince Ranier and Grace Kelly's wedding. Daddy and I talked about how pretty Grace was, then he said, "Wilda, you could marry a prince someday if you wanted to—you could have *anyone* you wanted!"

It was such an incidental comment, but I've found that the most profound truths are sometimes hidden in such statements.

I had always wanted lots of money. I believed that a person with lots of money would have absolutely no problems, except deciding where to spend it! When I married, I wanted my children to have plenty so that they wouldn't have to go through what I had as a child.

For some reason (and who can figure out the mind of a sixteen-year-old girl?), that Grace Kelly picture and my dad's encouragement showed me that I had gotten sidetracked with Blaine. He wasn't the kind of person who would give me what I wanted.

So I knew I had to call it quits. To everyone else at school, my decision was certainly not earth-shattering, but to me it was a monumental decision between a jealous young man and a life in which I would make something of myself.

Knowing that didn't make anything easier. I thought that the day I broke up with Blaine would be the saddest day of my life. I had made up my mind that I wouldn't give up my dreams—not for Blaine or anybody else—so I talked myself into telling him, and met him in the park.

It was like a plot from a grade "B" movie—us sitting on the grass under a gigantic, overshadowing tree—two teenagers in love, with one about to spring the "so long" song on the other:

"I've got to tell you something..."

When I finished, he just turned and walked away. I've wondered since what my life would have been like had I called Blaine back (if I could have spoken with my throat choking back the sobs).

Maybe I would have weakened if I had continued seeing him around school and town, but he called me not long after we broke up—"I've enlisted in the army, and I'm gonna go take the physical exam."

It was like a knife in my heart. Now I wouldn't even be able to see him. I agreed to meet him one last time the night after his physical. But the night of our date, I got a phone call. The army had shipped Blaine directly from his physical examination center to boot camp. He wouldn't be home for six weeks, and six weeks is an eternity to a teenager. So he was gone out of my life—if not forever, at least long enough to get over the hurt a sixteen-year-old girl feels.

But I was determined never again to live through the misery I went through as a child.

Chapter Seven

Bill

In my senior year of high school, I got a job at a little family-owned drive-in restaurant called the "Toot'n Tell 'em." It was like a scene right out of *"Happy Days"* with the waitresses going out to the cars with trays of 'burgers and cokes for greasy-haired guys and bleached-blonde girls in their '53 Mercurys and '57 Chevys. It was a crazy mix of teenage antics and rock 'n roll music and the few wary adults who ventured in.

I loved working there—not just that I was around everyone, but because I liked having my own money...my own clothes, perfumes, magazines. I could buy my own lunches at school. I was thrilled with the experience of being independent and earning my *own* money. Some weekends I could earn twenty-five dollars in tips alone—a smile, a kind voice, plus good service equals tips! It gave me confidence on how to make and manage money. I even paid the down-payment on my parents' first television.

And I became more ambitious. I tried out for the all-county chorus and was one of only five selected from my school. Then I won the "Snow Queen" title at school—socially, it was a really high honor. I found it easier and easier to make friends as I moved up the "success" ladder.

There were no other boys I got serious with after Blaine—that is, until...

It was December 27, 1958. I had been set up for a blind date, but was not looking forward to it at all. That afternoon, a friend dropped by to advise me to break my date that night—"He has such a horrible reputation as a Don Juan—kissing and telling, you know, and worse!" I decided quickly that I wouldn't be the subject for his sordid conquest stories.

So I asked my mother to call and break the date. Then I called my sister, Carol, at her job in Charleston and asked her to meet me for a movie that night.

Snow was filtering down that afternoon, but West Virginians don't take snow seriously until it really begins to accumulate.

I had the plans all made, so I went ahead and caught the Charleston-bound bus. But the snow slowed the bus enough that when I did get to the Charleston terminal, Carol and her friend had gotten tired of waiting (maybe figured I had gone ahead with the blind date) and went on to the movie.

So, there I was—a small-town, seventeen-year-old girl all by myself in the "big city" at night. After waiting to see if they would come back for me, I ran across the street to a little diner to try to catch a glimpse of Carol. While crossing the street, I noticed two men following me. I was already a bit frightened that Carol wasn't there to meet me, so my fright increased quickly as I remembered all the stories about girls getting picked up in the city.

My eyes skimmed nervously over all the faces in the diner's chrome booths. When I couldn't see Carol, I ran back across the street into the safety of the bus terminal. When I sat down—sure enough— the two young men sat down across from me. I was almost out of earshot, but I could tell from their barely audible voices that they were talking about me.

I was very shy, so I'm sure my face turned beet red when a few moments later the youngest of the two walked over, laid a napkin beside me, then walked over to the cigarette machine.

My ears heard the jingling of coins and the soft thump of cigarettes hitting the machine tray, but my eyes went back to the napkin. On it—obviously scrawled in haste—were the words:

"You are so pretty. I'd love to know your name. Please don't be offended, but I just can't help commenting on your beauty."

It was signed, "Bill."

When I looked up, I looked into his warm, green eyes. Then I saw his face and that big, broad, beautiful smile (here we go again with another scene

44

from a movie), and all I could do was smile back. When I did, he took it as a signal that he could sit down beside me. The other man (I later found out that it was Bill's brother) left.

My initial reaction of nervousness left just as quickly. Bill was so unassuming—no pressure. I realized soon that he was more little boy than masher.

We talked for a long time—our families, birthdays, schools...then he asked if he could take me for a drive. Tenseness again! I told him in no uncertain terms that I didn't get in cars with perfect strangers.

"Okay," he countered, "how about some window shopping?"

He was so easy to talk with, so unlike any of the other young men that I had dated. We walked for blocks talking about the window displays, the fashions, the clothes we liked.

I lost track of time. When we got back to the terminal, Carol was there, too. Bill wanted to take us home, but we told him "no." I figured as we waved goodbye that I wouldn't see him again. It had been fun, but...he did ask for my telephone number; then the Greyhound sped into the night.

The next morning I went to my grandmother's house to go to church with her. In jest I said, "Grandma, I met my future husband last night!"

Grandmother asked what I meant, saying, "Oh, honey, you must be careful—there are such bad men out there wanting to lead you on, especially in the big city."

"Not Bill," I argued. "He has such an innocent face."

Grandma just laughed at my "passing fancy." Then we left for church. When we got back to her house, the phone was ringing—it was Bill.

"Hi! Your mother gave me your grandmother's number. Hope you don't mind that I called..."

We dated the following Saturday night—a double date with Carol and her boyfriend. Four Saturday nights later we went out alone.

Daddy wasn't comfortable about my new boyfriend. Bill was 23, and I was only 17. Daddy felt I was still too young to get serious. He also knew that I had some special dreams and plans.

I did ask Bill about his plans and if he was a Christian. "Yes," he spoke openly, "I've gone down to the altar during revivals several times—I've even been baptized three times."

Bill believed that he could "fall from grace" when he sinned, and instead of praying for forgiveness, he thought he had to get saved all over again. I didn't understand that part of his beliefs but was satisfied that we agreed on all the rest.

Bill was so kind and gentle. He was a lot of fun to be around, and I could see that my affection could easily turn to love.

My relationship with Bill was like a chapter in a storybook—before long I was swept completely off my feet. It was the kind of thing that song lyrics have been made of since the time men and women began singing love songs to each other.

Then one night the perfect picture was torn to fragmented shreds. We went to a movie, and I could sense that Bill was nervous about something. On the way home, he stopped by his little apartment, and told me to stay in the car, saying, "I've got something inside that I want you to see."

I figured that it was a surprise and went along with the lark. It could even be some type of practical joke—Bill was always doing funny things.

When he came back outside, he had pictures of two little blonde-haired girls. I looked at them and shrugged, "Who are they?"

With short breaths, he began unraveling a story that I found so hard to believe. When he was only seventeen, he had met a girl named Tina. They dated during their junior year in high school, then she found that she was pregnant with Bill's child. Feeling it was the most honorable thing to do, he married her, and within two years they were the parents of not only one, but two girls—the blonde ones smiling in the pictures.

But, he explained further, it was a mistake from the beginning. Everyone involved knew it, and they were divorced before either reached their twenty-first birthday.

Tina had remarried shortly after the divorce was finalized, and the lawyers had talked Bill into giving up the little girls for adoption to her new husband—"for the good of the children, you know."

Bill went on to explain that his mother, Nell, had been hurt deeply by her husband who had not told her about a previous marriage of his own until after their wedding. So, during the months that I had been dating Bill, Nell kept threatening to tell me about the divorce if he didn't. She had insisted that he tell me everything and take his chances—especially that he not date me any longer under false pretenses.

It was so sad as Bill and I sat there that night in the car outside his apartment—Bill, me, the pictures of his little babies. I could tell that his heart was still broken over losing his children. All he had left of them was a little stuffed animal, a few pictures, and overflowing bad memories.

But even though my heart ached for him, and though I knew that he was hurting, I couldn't bring myself to help him. It was just too much for me to handle. I was only a month away from my eighteenth birthday, and he was—well, not at all like I thought he had been.

He looked like the Ivy League college-type, so innocent and clean-cut, not like a divorced father of two children. It didn't make sense.

In an instant, he had changed from a man I knew I loved to a man who seemed the opposite of my ideal husband.

Quite frankly, I had been taught that virginity was a prized possession—that if I was a virgin on my wedding night that my husband would cherish and honor and respect me the rest of my life.

I had always believed that a moral, pure girl was the ideal of all men. In return, I expected the same thing in the man I married—that he be moral and pure.

All along I had dreamed that I would fall in love with some handsome "prince" who would also wait for the wedding night. We would present ourselves to each other, and we'd share that special first time together. I wanted my husband and me to explore, adventure, and learn together.

It was part of the whole American dream.

But my dream had been shattered by Bill's startling revelation. Suddenly he was so...different. He had made love with another woman. He had fathered two children with her. Our children could never be his first. He seemed so used—not the "prince charming" he had been as he bounded up the apartment steps just minutes before.

I asked him to drive me home, and silently as the headlights pierced the night, I began piecing my thoughts together. Part of me still loved him, still wanted to be with him, still saw him as an innocent young man. But another part of me was hurt and defensive and never wanted to see him again. I knew what people would say about me—dating a divorced man. It was 1959 and divorce was extremely taboo, especially in our area.

The part that didn't want to see him again won my inward struggle. I decided to quit dating him and told him so as we talked in my driveway. As we walked to the door, he handed me a note, got back in the car, and left.

My anger flared when I read, "When you grow up, please call me." "Me!" I thought, "you are the one who messed everything up!" Crumpling the paper, I stomped into the house. As far as I was concerned, when I tossed the paper into the trash can, it was the last remnant of Bill Marple's life that I ever wanted to see. I wanted nothing more to do with him—ever!

That worked fine, at least until several weeks later when Bill pulled into the "Toot 'n Tell'em" in a sparkling-new, black and red Austin-Healey. The sports car was his excuse to come over, but I could tell from the twinkle in his eyes that he had an ulterior motive.

Inwardly, I was so glad to see him—too glad in fact—my heart was beating a mile-a-minute. I tried to keep calm and aloof, even when looking at his car.

His ulterior motive was an invitation to a big concert in Charleston the next weekend. He knew that music was my weakness. Before he left that night, I had agreed to go with him—"just one more time!"

I looked at the car as he buzzed down the road, then glanced down at his tray. There, spelled out

with torn bits of drinking straw, were the words—
"*I Love You.*" It was the perfect, corny, romantic
touch that I liked so much about Bill.

That concert date led to another. Then another.
I felt myself falling harder than ever. Bill—despite
his "tainted" past—was perfect for me in so many
ways.

One night Daddy asked me who I was going
out with. I said, "Bill," as innocently as I could—I
was so afraid that he knew something that I wasn't
about to tell him. Well, he didn't know then, but my
fears were realized shortly afterwards. Carol heard
about Bill while on her job in Charleston and was
very concerned about me, so concerned that she told
my mother.

The story was out—Mother talked to Daddy
alone, then he needed time to think about it. It
was—all in all—the three longest days of my life. In
the end, I was given my parent's permission to date
Bill—with reservations on their part.

Daddy came past me while I was brushing my
hair one night not long after. I don't know what was
going through his mind (maybe he was seeing his
little ragamuffin girl once again—now so grown-
up), but he grinned—"Wilda Sue, you're really
working hard to get Bill aren't you?"

I smiled back. Daddy thought for a moment,
then concluded, "Well, once you get him, you'll
have to work twice as hard to keep him."

That seemed to be Daddy's official stamp of

approval. He never said another discouraging word about my relationship with Bill again.

I didn't know where this dream for my "prince charming" would end. The dream had been slightly tarnished—it was true—but it was still alive. At least for the moment, it seemed perfectly right to fall in love with my Bill.

Chapter Eight

Miss West Virginia

Daddy always seemed wise concerning his children. He wanted us all to be beautiful and happy. He was proud of the fact that his girls primped, joking, "Any ole barn looks better with a little paint!"

So he was especially proud when one of the producers for the Miss West Virginia Beauty Pageant called him. Someone felt that I had a good chance and wanted to sponsor me in the upcoming pageant.

After the producer and my daddy talked, an approval was signed, and I was officially entered in the contest.

Life suddenly became a small collection of whirlwinds—preparation, dress fittings, practicing. Finally, the night arrived. The auditorium in Charleston was filled with excited, anxious hundreds. Backstage was a maze of nerves. The audience and the contestants all knew that the night could be the beginning of dreams fulfilled for one girl—only one. The tension was suffocating.

I won the talent division singing and playing the guitar—a country favorite, "Release Me." By that time, I had become numb with the excitement of participating with so many talented, beautiful girls.

Then the big moment arrived. Suddenly the swishing of taffeta gowns hushed. We held our breath for what seemed an eternity. I heard my name, but the entire sequence spiraled like a dream around me. I was bathed in lights. The tiara was placed on my bouffant hairdo. All-American tears were streaming down my cheeks. I remember so little from the next moments—the congratulations, hugs from the other contestants, music, fanfare. It would take days for the reality of that crowning moment to sink in. I could hardly believe that I would be representing my home state in the Miss USA Pageant—the preliminaries for the Miss Universe Contest. But the newspaper headlines the next morning confirmed what seemed like a dream— *Wilda Sue Estep, Crowned 1959 Miss West Virginia!!*

That incredible night was just the beginning of a faster swirling summer to come. After weeks of training, shopping (part of the Miss West Virginia winnings included clothing), and umpteen hours of packing/unpacking/packing, I was flown on my first airplane ride to Long Beach, California.

On the plane trip to California, I kept thinking of the people back home in West Virginia. It had been such a beautiful time at the Charleston airport—hundreds of people had come for a going-away party. Before I had boarded the plane for Long Beach, I had looked out at my daddy and mother, my sisters and Jerry, my friends, and my relatives, the pageant officials—I couldn't see Bill, but later found out that his boss wouldn't let him off. As I waved to that crowd from the plane entrance, I wondered if everything would be the same when I returned. I also wondered if I would ever be the same again.

The non-stop whirlwind began the moment the plane touched down in Long Beach. For starters, I was greeted by Miss Welcome of Long Beach—she thought I was a contestant from South America. Then I was chosen from all the other contestants to be the Penney's Queen (a title sponsored by the J. C. Penney Company). That company lavished me with presents and a wardrobe of new clothing from their stores; in return, I was used by them for publicity and the promotion of their products.

Talk about a fish out of water—I couldn't have felt farther out of my element. It was the last year that the Miss USA and Miss Universe pageants were held jointly, so I felt like a little barefoot hillbilly in the midst of a chic array of the world's most beautiful girls.

Imagine my shock when most of the other girls felt exactly the same way—out of their class—and we all became very close, very quickly. That helped my wavering self-esteem some, but as the two-week adventure began, I still wondered what in the world I was doing in such a high-class event.

My roommate at the LaFayette Hotel was Miss South Carolina—Mary Ann Powell, also a born-again Christian. Like me (and all the other girls), she confided that she felt so out of place.

But we had little time for reflection, fears, or congeniality. Every waking moment was spent practicing routines and being honored by dignitaries. The first night we were ushered into a gigantic ballroom replete with huge glistening, crystal chandeliers hanging from the ceiling, each of us escorted by a Naval Academy cadet from our home state. I felt like Cinderella. After that, we were guests of honor in two giant parades with each of us in lavish floats.

At the city ceremony, each contestant brought a gift from her state for the mayor. I brought a cuff-link/tie-clasp set made from coal. In return, the mayor presented a shimmering gold key to the city to each of us. As part of that ceremony, each contestant wore a costume reflecting something from their state—a hillbilly girl/Daisy Mae outfit for me— what else?

That night, after we were transported back to our hotel, I knew something was happening to me. From that moment on, I felt the glare of numerous eyes and began to notice that there were increasing numbers of talent scouts and movie producers around me.

I surprised myself at how well I was able to conceal my inner feelings and questions. I had gained a lot of confidence in myself through the Miss West Virginia Pageant. I had heard a quote— "Nothing succeeds like success." If those judges felt that I had talent and looks, then I must be a little special at least.

A new dream was developing, and it was the beginning of a lot of changes for me. I really did begin to believe that I was becoming a beauty queen.

The night before the competition actually began, the contestants all performed individual talent routines during a star-studded show. I loved the applause as I finished "Release Me," but more than that, I felt overwhelmed to hear the other girls sing and play and dance—there was so much talent there.

Then—shock! The next night, I heard what seemed impossible—I had been chosen from all of the contestants to be one of the top finalists.

But I didn't have the time or energy to ponder what the selection meant. I was too numb with excitement at the swirl of attention and activity.

From the time I was picked among the headliners, I began to receive telegrams and phone calls from talent scouts—not just from Hollywood, but from other places as well. They offered jobs (one was to be a showgirl at the Las Vegas *Tropicana Hotel*) and screen tests (some even went ahead and arranged tests without asking me).

Things were moving so fast—I wanted to stay

in control and enjoy the pageant, but my head was spinning. In just a couple of days, I had been literally whisked away from my little Elkview, West Virginia, and placed among enough glitter to drown anyone!

The next day I was taken to the Columbia Studios in Hollywood where they were filming "Who Was That Lady?" Within minutes after my arrival, I was placed between Tony Curtis and Dean Martin! It was a scene that was so dream-like, but those were their real arms around me, and those were real cameras snapping. Imagine—me between two of the most glamorous movie stars in the world!

Even as they were taking my picture with those giant stars, I heard some of the studio people talking—planning a publicity campaign built around me. I'm sure that at least some of the other contestants were getting similar attention, but for me—it was as though I had stepped into a make-believe world. When I had been a bit younger, I had a picture of Rhonda Fleming on a calendar above my bed, and often I would look up at her, dreaming that I would someday be beautiful and glamorous and rich and happy like she seemed to be. Could my dreams really be coming true?

Yet, the most amazing thing of all that day in the studio was that I was so unimpressed with the quality of people I saw there. So many of the "biggies" and stars that I met during the next few hours seemed so bored and dissatisfied with what they were doing. They seemed as ungenuine as the fake storefronts on the movie lots that I saw.

I should have been overwhelmed by the contacts I was making, but I couldn't help seeing the same look I had seen in my father's eyes back in the old days—longing, hungry, searching, empty.

During the next few days, in-between the parties, festivities, and publicity sessions, something very strange happened. A woman showed up and asked for me; I had never seen her before, but she seemed to know me. She was dressed in the finest clothing, was dripping with diamonds, and was so sure of herself.

She said that she was Mrs. Susan Calloway (not her real name). She claimed to be a relative, and from the beginning seemed to have my entire life mapped out for me. I checked with Daddy and found that she was indeed a cousin of his. She had read the newsprint about the pageant, made the connection that I was her relative, and decided to guide my career. (It wasn't really a career yet, but a lot of people were saying that I had a great future ahead in Hollywood.) She had read about the screen tests some of the contestants had been offered and wanted me to come and live at her house after the two weeks were over. From her description of the smartly decorated rooms, and the luxurious pool, it was no "holler" shack either!

Mrs. Calloway called my dad and told him of her plans. The West Virginia media had been running stories on all my activities, so my family was already excited about the screen tests and offers. Daddy immediately gave his approval for me to stay with her. She, in return, was certain that I would snap up the opportunity—after all, who wouldn't jump at the chance (even if it was only a chance) to be tomorrow's Rhonda Fleming or Elizabeth Taylor?

But there was something about her "you-poor-little - ole - hillbilly - girl - come - to - Hollywood - with - stars - in - your - eyes" routine that I didn't like. It was as if her money and pool lifestyle were being dangled like steaks before me. I knew that there had to be a price tag somewhere.

In the meantime, the Miss USA Pageant drew to a close. I was a frontrunner to the very end, but wasn't picked among the top five finalists. I was far from disappointed—I was still too much in shock from being named among the headliners.

Then, too, there was the upcoming Twentieth Century-Fox screen test that had been arranged by an ambitious talent scout. Everyone concerned felt it was a cinch for me to land a part—in fact, newspapers had already leaked a release back to West Virginia, that I was being tested opposite Fabian in Twentieth Century's "Hound Dog Man!"

So I knew that it wasn't just a pipe-dream. That made my choices concerning the screen test, Mrs. Calloway, and my entire life crucially important.

The post-pageant festivities continued during

the remainder of the second week, and the day of the big test came quickly. The night before I was scheduled to go to the studio was agony—I spent it tossing and turning in my bed. I knew that I was going to be offered the chance of a lifetime—the opportunity to not only become a movie starlet (if I could believe what the agents and studio people were saying), but also a way to escape the poverty of my childhood. All my life had been spent dreaming of just such an opportunity.

Somehow, that night, when confronted with such a monumental decision, I found a wisdom much advanced for my years. Without experiencing the emptiness I saw in those stars' eyes, I knew that I didn't want to go that way—no matter how tempting the possible offers.

By morning, I knew that I had no desire to go through with the screen test. It was all so much hype. For one thing, even though I considered myself a singer, I knew that I wasn't trained to be an actress. The bottom line was this—they didn't want me for a part opposite Fabian because of my acting talent. In a business built on cheesecake and sex, innocent-looking girls were unusual, perhaps, but I wasn't dumb enough to believe that *used* innocent-looking girls weren't a dime-a-dozen (and Hollywood has absolutely no use for "has-beens").

When I made it to the top, it would be in my own territory and on my own terms—it would be because I had earned the success, not just because I was an empty-headed beauty who happened to be at the right place at the right time. My success would be hard-fought, perhaps, but it would last because I would deserve it.

That morning I announced my decision—I was not interested in the screen test or in life in Southern California. My newfound friends were incredulous—many of them had an ultimate desire to be "discovered" while in California.

Mrs. Calloway, Twentieth Century-Fox, my friends, and my family at home notwithstanding—I knew that I had made the right decision. When it was made, I felt wonderfully free from the fake, unreal, tainted world that I had seen.

The memories I had made making pictures and headlines in the movie capital of the world would last forever, but I knew more than ever that I didn't want to trust a dream that would fluff away before I could taste it. My dreams—whatever they would be—were going to be built on real things.

When I returned, my family thought I had gone totally bonkers. The papers had been carrying all the "local girl makes good" stories, so they thought I was well on my way to a movie or television career. Imagine their surprise when I called and said that I was taking the next plane home! If only I could have shared all my thoughts with them, especially about some of the things I had seen.

I knew that the pace would not let up when I got back home—my reign as Miss West Virginia was just beginning, and I was expected to travel all over the state during the coming year. I was surprised, however, that more movie and show business offers kept coming. One that I remember distinctly was from a producer in South America, Herman Jesson—a long letter commenting about my black hair and beauty, calling me "the prettiest girl in the USA," and offering me a part in a film opposite the 1958 Miss Universe.

I kept this and the other cards and telegram offers, but refused all of them except one—a marriage proposal from Bill!

Chapter Nine

Dreams That Count

After I arrived home from the beauty pageant, Bill told me that he had ordered something while I was in California. When he flashed a beautiful diamond ring, it wasn't a hard decision for me to accept. The time spent apart had been hard for both of us—we realized then more than ever how much our love had grown. So I said, "Yes!", but felt we should wait for a year before we got married. I still had my Miss West Virginia contracts to fulfill.

The remaining summer months were filled with traveling all over—to special events, parades, conventions, fairs. I must have flashed a zillion smiles and waved to another zillion people, but I enjoyed every minute of the reign.

However, there was one thing that I soon found out—traveling was not without problems. One weekend in Parkersburg was the breaking point. I was to ride in a parade, sing on a radio program, and meet country music star Jim Ed Brown. Everything went without incident, but the problems started when I went to my room that night.

I had a chaperone—she was in her early twenties—who stayed with me. Our room was across the hall from the producer's room. Bill stayed with the producer that night since he had been able to make the Parkersburg trip with me.

Well, my chaperone was in and out all night. It seemed that she had "something going" with some of the conventioneers who were staying in the same hotel. I don't know if she knew I was aware that she was "turning tricks" or not, but I would have to have been awfully naive not to know what was going on.

Bill was like my bodyguard—keeping watch over me. He knew what was going on, too, since the chaperone's reputation had spread quickly through the motel. He stayed up all night at his door to make sure that my chaperone didn't bring men into my room. He wanted to keep me safe.

That was just the beginning. On subsequent trips, my chaperone obviously made a nice amount of money during afterhours. Bill wasn't able to make all the trips, so I pretty well had to fend for myself when he wasn't there.

I got so fed up with it. One day I joked with Bill, "We should go ahead and get married—at least I'd feel safe if you were my chaperone!"

It was really meant to be a joke, but Bill jumped on the idea like a "hen on a Junebug!"

Both of us were pretty impulsive, so together we were even more so. Within days, we gave the big announcement to our families and friends. Within a few weeks, we set the date—September 1, 1959.

We both knew that I wasn't supposed to get married until I crowned the next Miss West Virginia, but I knew that they wouldn't take my title since I had already represented the state in the Miss USA Pageant.

Bill and I also knew that I should have gone ahead and finished high school before getting married, as we had originally planned. I was eighteen and should have already graduated, but since I had failed the second grade, I was one year behind for my age.

Naturally, my parents weren't overjoyed about the wedding plans, but they could see that we were determined. On the first day of September, we were married in a little country church not far from my family's home. It was just a small wedding—we didn't have the time or money for elaborate plans.

Then we were off on our honeymoon in Virginia Beach, Virginia, and the beautiful beginning of a life together.

Life was moving so fast—the past few months had been like I was on a top that was spinning so rapidly that I could hardly see around me. Everything was so blurred. The roller-coaster ride kept going faster and faster.

We got back from our short honeymoon with

just enough time to move into our little upstairs apartment before I had to enroll in Charleston's Stonewall Jackson High School for my senior year.

The pace quickened—being a married girl, traveling to my Miss West Virginia engagements, going to a new high school, doing homework, cooking for my new husband—what a curious mix!

Three months later, Bill decided that we should buy our first little home. We found the perfect one in South Charleston. What a dream—especially for the little holler girl that still lived inside me.

The move to our new home entailed changing schools. However, with having to pick colors, drapes, carpet, and all the "important" things, I just didn't see how I could continue going to school, so I took the equivalency test. In short order, I passed the test, received my diploma, and never went back to school.

At least that helped ease my hectic schedule some, but by that time I was starting to take some modeling jobs around Charleston. The sessions paid well, especially because of the Miss West Virginia title, and the modeling checks would keep coming during the next five years.

The modeling also provided some "unusual" opportunities. One was for a big convention at the prestigious White Sulphur Springs Hotel. I got the call to do a large fashion show, but I also found that one of my "obligations" was to serve orange juice each morning in one of the executive suites—to one of the top officials in his bedroom! I was flabbergasted that they would even suggest such a thing (and even more flabbergasted that some of the other models played the game for all it was worth). I cancelled that particular contract, post-haste.

But that was mild compared to the photo arts studio—the job was supposed to be a model for a photo contest. When I arrived at the specified time and place, I asked for my wardrobe. They replied that there was none. It was a nude contest. Quick tracks again!

Life as a whole was a lark. Even with the whirlwind schedule, I was doing things that I loved. I was playing house and making friends with my new neighbors. I drank my very first cup of coffee at a neighborhood get-together one morning; the other women must have gotten a real kick out of watching me trying to be grown-up and sophisticated.

I had led a sheltered life—school, home and protective father, church, working at a small, neighborhood drive-in restaurant. What a difference a few months had made! Being a beauty queen and getting married to Bill radically changed my life. But, through all of the excitement, I didn't see how much I was changing on the inside.

Bill's job at Union Carbide's Technical Center entailed lots of parties for the employees. Like most young newlyweds, we were thrilled to be accepted at such "grown-up" activities and didn't miss one. It was a shock, at first, to see how everyone else drank at the parties. But after the first few tastes, it didn't seem quite so bad. I even tried cigarettes. I couldn't believe that I had been against them both for so many years. It wasn't nearly as bad as I thought it would be—kind of fun in fact.

Truthfully, the parties stimulated me—made me feel so adult and urban. I couldn't wait for the next one. I would spend hours shopping for a new dress each time another party was coming up.

It seemed that we didn't have as much time for church and family activities as we used to. We didn't plan to neglect them; we just didn't have as much time anymore.

By the time I crowned the new Miss West Virginia, my life had changed drastically. In the rush of pageant festivities that led to the moment when I placed the sparkling tiara on another stiffly sprayed hairdo, I had little time to reflect on the past year. I looked basically the same as the year before, but what a difference. One year before I had been the most innocent, blushing, naive girl as I was crowned Miss West Virginia. Out in the audience had been the most handsome prince I had ever laid eyes on—the man I was falling in love with.

It had only been 365 days, and indeed so many dreams had come true. I had seen the "world"; I was accepted, said to be beautiful, was married to the best man in the world, and was now preparing during the coming months to give my husband a baby. We were experiencing the joys of Suburbia,

USA, in our secure, little, three-bedroom home—complete with wall-to-wall carpeting and air-conditioning inside, patio with brick barbeque pit outside.

Bill was making a comfortable salary and was a good husband. If anything, the bad experience with his first marriage had made him even more loving, understanding, and romantic.

It was a dream world—pure and simple—my Great American Dream of 1960. Life couldn't have been more beautiful.

Dad and the Starlight Quartet before Ellen joined us. (l to r) Me, Joyce, Carol, Jerry and, of course, Dad. Little Ellen is playing in the creek in the background.

Grandmother's farm house in Lind's Fork Holler. We thought it was a mansion! *(Photo taken in 1981)*.

Mother, Bill, and me celebrating the night I won the Miss West Virginia title.

As I waved my good-byes on my way to Long Beach, I really wondered if I would ever be the same. *(Photo by West Virginia Publicity Commission.)*

My lil ole Daisy Mae outfit and the young seaman who escorted me to the pageant festivities. *(Official United States Navy Photograph.)*

Such an honor to be chosen as a top finalist in the Miss USA pageant! I'm in the bottom row, far right.

What a thrill, representing West Virginia in the
parade of floats!

Modeling jobs were fun and plentiful with my title as Miss West Virginia. *(Photo by Photo-Art Studio.)*

This was an opportunity to model sitting on the back of Bill's little Austin-Healey sports car.

**The most special dream of all —
my marriage to Bill.**
(Photo by Photo-Art Studio.)

Chapter Ten

First Years

Our son, Les, was born one year, two and a half months after we were married. It was election night, 1960, the night John Fitzgerald Kennedy was elected the new President of the United States.

Although my pregnancy had gone without a hitch, I had a horrible time with the delivery. The baby was late coming, so labor was finally induced.

It began at nine a.m. and continued all day and night. Bill and the doctor stayed in my room with me all night alternating between watching the election returns, comforting me, rubbing my back, and waiting for the coming movements. When it became apparent that the baby was coming breech, Dr. Lilly had to turn him inside me.

As the baby's shrill cries pierced the morning delivery room, I had little time to understand the full meaning of a new life coming into the world—I was in too much pain for much philosophic thought.

I found out quickly that no person is really ready to be a parent. It's the one job that there is little

71

preparation for, and when a person finally learns what it's all about, the child is grown. What an occupation!

But we loved it from the beginning. Les was our proverbial "pride and joy"—that's an understatement if ever there was one! We did all the usual things—the showers, the early morning feedings, the "oohs and ahhs" caused by miniature clothes. We took him everywhere, inwardly bursting with pride.

We were still "spur of the moment" people, but with the baby, the "spurs" took a little bit longer! It wasn't a perfect life, I suppose, but so close we didn't know the difference.

Then one morning it ended. It was 1962. Bill went off to work like he had hundreds of times, lunch in hand. By mid-morning he was standing in the doorway, lunch still in hand. I could tell by his face that something was horribly, irrevocably wrong.

Union Carbide had been cutting back and laying off workers—it had happened to several people we knew. One man had even committed suicide when the lifestyle that he had known ended abruptly. But we never dreamed that Bill would receive his "pink slip," too.

No book could ever describe the terror we felt as we sat huddled together that morning, wondering what would happen to us. In Charleston, West Virginia, Union Carbide was *the* place to work. It was *the* Chemical City of the world. Just about everyone we knew worked there.

We were heartbroken, and numb with fear. With the layoffs that had already happened, other jobs—even part-time positions—were totally non-existent in the entire Charleston area.

We had been living well during the years since we had been married, but we had also been living hand-to-mouth, just making it from check to check to be able to pay the bills on our new car, new house, new furniture, new clothes, and new baby. It didn't take an accountant to figure out that it would only take a week or two without a check to destroy the life we had built.

Bill went looking for a job immediately. He would come home each day with the usual bad news. Everyday he would encourage me, "There's a job out there somewhere—I just have to find it."

Finally, he got a job selling speculative stock. A couple of stockbrokers, Morris Miller and Pat Conner, saw potential in Bill and took him under their wing.

In the next six months, Bill proved their instincts right—he made $15,000. We started thinking that maybe losing his job at Union Carbide was a blessing in disguise.

Then, as soon as that fell in place, it fell apart. The economy tightened, and the bottom fell out of speculative stock. Bill tried to sell mutual funds and other items, but it wasn't like before. In a short time, we went through the money he had made.

During the next two years, he received a full-blown education in the school of "hard knocks." How he survived is a total miracle—lots of men in his shoes gave up.

We had little money coming in and were continually "robbing Peter to pay Paul." It didn't take long for us to realize just how fragile the Great American Dream had been. The roller coaster ride we had been on for two years was about to crash—we both saw the inevitable. We got further and further behind in house payments, car payments, gasoline payments—where would it end?

Bill's car was repossessed—how embarrassing! His mother donated a $200 "oldie but goodie" jalopy, but at least he had something to drive. Then, we had to sell our dream home to try to pay our way out of debt. I cried all day the day the house was sold; I could see me ending up in a holler shack again!

All of a sudden we looked around and had nothing—no friendly suburban neighbors, no shining goodies, no electronic necessities, no furniture. We just had ourselves, and without all the trappings that seemed pretty bleak.

Bill was able to pick up a little money here and there, so we were able to at least rent a little house where we would eventually live for almost two years.

One night when we got down to the last bite of

food in the house and no money for more—it really hit me. I went in and heated the few leftovers in an aluminum plate, sat that plate before Les for him to eat, and went into another room so Les and Bill wouldn't see me crying.

I hated it! Despised it! It wasn't just that we had gone from barbeques, patios, and suburban living down to nothing, but all those childhood memories were being conjured up—the hunger, loneliness, and bleak existence. When I saw Les eating the last bit of food in the house, I had the same numb, sick feeling that I had lived with continually as a little holler girl. I was poor and dumb and rejected again. I had little to call my own and not much hope for the future. I was still that six-year-old ragamuffin who stood beside the road counting cars instead of participating in the Easter Egg hunt. It was just that almost two decades had passed.

I became very depressed, lost my appetite and twenty-five pounds. I couldn't sleep, and one night I was listening to the TV until it signed off. Just as the flag was waving and some faceless band was playing "Taps," I heard a voice say, "You're going to die before you reach twenty-five!"

I looked around but no one was there. Bill and Les were both asleep. Fear gripped my heart much like what I had seen in my mother when she was "cursed" by that practicing witch when we were children. For all my "sophistication," I was little different. The next two years were a living nightmare of fear-filled dreams—eerie sequences of musty funeral flowers and Bill holding Les as my casket was lowered into the ground.

All the pain—the layoff, the shattered middle-class dreams, the grimness of life crashing down on us, the death-voice—all of it seemed so final. Somehow, someway I just hoped that there would be a light at the end of this bleak tunnel.

Chapter Eleven

The Dream That Cost $31.50

In 1963, not long after the "world caved in," I was asked to attend a cosmetics demonstration. It was fun being with the other women and talking about lipsticks and perfume, but when I was asked to consider becoming a beauty consultant, Bill refused. "I'm not having any wife of mine go around door-to-door selling makeup!" he said bluntly. "I will do the working. I want my wife at home."

So I let the subject drop, even though as bad times got worse, we could have used the extra money—any extra money.

Then during May, 1965, I went with a girlfriend to another demonstration. I didn't have any money to buy cosmetics, but I was always interested in beauty aids, so I went mostly out of curiosity. While there, the consultant, Marge, commented, "You know, Wilda Sue, you'd make a great beauty consultant." I didn't have the heart to tell her that she was the second woman from the same company

77

to say that, nor did I tell her what my husband had said the other time. However, I did agree to have her hold a show in my house, and I did take home some of the literature on becoming a beauty consultant.

When I returned, I laid the sales manual down and forgot about it, but Bill picked it up the next day and began reading it, page by page. Then, I saw him writing figures on paper. During the days before the appointment with Marge, he read and reread the literature.

Marge was so wise—she had instantly sized up the situation—Bill's hostility to me becoming a consultant. On the night of the makeup party in my home, she waited until the other women had left and Bill came home. Then she started telling both of us about the opportunities for me in Fashion Two-Twenty.

She told us about the company that V. G. Gochneaur started on February 20, 1962. John Glenn had also made his historic flight that same day, so Mr. Gochneaur honored the two events by calling his company Fashion Two-Twenty (2/20/62). The quality line of cosmetics and high volume of business created the demand for a multi-million dollar plant in Aurora, Ohio. The large profit margins that Mr. G. offered to his growing number of consultants, managers, and studio owners was one reason for the rapid rise. The company's growth eventually had led to international circulation, but Marge explained that there were still some areas in the United States that were untouched by the fledgling, self-starting business.

Marge had done so well with the company that she and her husband were moving to Greensboro, North Carolina, soon to open their own training and distribution center.

I looked over at Bill while Marge continued talking. She had his attention, so she kept giving him more information. She said that I had a lot of potential, and suggested that we move to Greensboro with them and get in on the "ground floor" in that new area.

By the time she left that night, she had Bill completely hooked. During the next few days, he went over and visited the Fashion Two-Twenty Studio in south Charleston and talked with Doy and Lucy Jones, the studio owners there.

He started talking about the business all the time, "Honey, you'd be a natural at it—it's not selling door-to-door or anything like I thought!" I could tell that he saw the potential in business terms as well: "It's the best opportunity I've ever seen, and I know you'd be good at it."

Unfortunately, I was no longer all that excited about becoming a beauty consultant. For one thing, I was sick; I had just found out that I was pregnant again. (Les was five at the time.) Not only was I having to cope with that familiar queasiness, but I was living in fear as I kept remembering how painful that torture-filled twenty-four hour delivery had been with Les.

And yet, at the same time, I was so totally unhappy with the way that we were living. Bill was doing as well as he possibly could, but the Charleston area was still in a slump from the huge Carbide lay-off. We both knew that we needed to go where there were more opportunities. I wanted something better, especially with another baby coming. The last three years had been a living nightmare, and I didn't want to spend another day like that if I didn't have to.

When Marge and Howard went to Greensboro to look for a studio site and an apartment, Bill decided to go along—"Just to look around."

When Bill got back from Greensboro, he hit me with the big news. He had rented a little house! I guess the non-stop encouragement from Marge and Howard, coupled with the dead-end street in Charleston, had done it.

While Bill and His brother, Perry, scurried about packing our few belongings in a rented truck, Les and I went over to see my parents to break the bittersweet news that we were leaving.

On the Fourth of July weekend, 1965, we hooked a trailer to the little jalopy that Bill's mother had given us and took off for "parts unknown." (Bill and Perry had taken the furniture to Greensboro the weekend before.)

Greensboro, North Carolina, was not nearly as forboding as I had pictured in my mind. It had been a small mill town in the past but had grown into a bustling center with a number of mostly textile-related industries.

As soon as we got settled in our cozy house (that sounds better than just saying "tiny"), I found a doctor to help me with my sickness. The pills he prescribed at least reduced the extreme nausea I was feeling from the pregnancy.

Bill began looking around for a job for himself, and in the meantime took me to Marge and Howard's new studio for their grand opening. That same day I signed a contract to become a beauty consultant. I had no idea what was ahead for me.

I began the training sessions, studying my sales manual for hours at a time.

I decided that—regardless of the way I felt or looked (increasingly pregnant)—I was *going* to be successful at my new business. Marge helped me to see that the sky was the limit—that I could make as much money as I was willing to work for.

I knew that I was willing to work as many hours as it took to make lots of money. I wanted a lot. I was sick and tired of being dirt-poor. The taste of the Great American Dream during our first three years of marriage had been just tantalizing enough to make my childhood hatred of poverty grow to a seething rage.

I figured that if I could make a lot of money, and as Bill got started in his portrait selling business—together we could buy our own home again, buy new things, and be happy. My dreams weren't that big—but they were material.

My first showcase cost a whopping $31.50—which I didn't have—so Marge and Howard let me pay them back during the next few weeks from my profits.

Quite frankly, there were many reasons why I shouldn't succeed, and the list seemed to grow more ominous:

I didn't have a car...I didn't have a telephone to make appointments for shows (the telephone company required a large installation fee which we didn't have)...I was pregnant...It was the last of the summer and was hot and muggy...I didn't know anybody, thus didn't know where or with whom to start...

Well, I figured that since the picture was so bleak, anything I did would be positive. Call it pluckiness or ignorant bliss or whatever—I walked over to the nearest housing development and began doing a survey. Maybe they felt sorry for this wilted-looking, pregnant woman or something, I don't know, but most of the women that were home let me come in and ask a few questions about cosmetics. From those initial surveys, I was able to book my first appointments.

The first week, I booked thirteen appointments for the rest of the month. The studio owners were amazed when I sold over $1000 that first month—not nearly as amazed as I was!

I held my first appointment on August 12th, and on October 1st, I was promoted to a manager! Then the owners told me that if I could keep up the pace of $1500 a month for six months and recruit six other women during the same time period, I could win a brand new company car.

Well, after beating the sizzling sidewalks and staggering over gravel pavements on swollen ankles, the possibility of winning a new car was like holding a chilled glass of Perrier in front of a thirsty man in the desert. I made up my mind that I would do it—no matter what it took!

I started talking about the business to every woman who would listen—in the laundromat, the grocery store, anywhere.

Bill began to get even more excited about Fashion Two-Twenty, too. Since he had gone to work selling a family album and portrait plan, he would also bring home names of women he had met who were interested in learning to better apply makeup. He also kept a list of ladies who were looking for a job opportunity where they could set their own hours.

I kept on like a "house a'fire" even though my pregnancy was getting more pronounced. Six months after I went with Fashion Two-Twenty, on February 4, 1966 (also Bill's birthday), I gave birth to our second son. We named him David, and unlike Les' delivery, this baby came with absolutely no complications. Whew! It must have been all that walking!

Two months after David's birth—eight months after I went with the company—I qualified for my first company car, a new Chevrolet Impala. The sparkling automobile just helped me realize how big the opportunities were. My dreams grew with the realization.

I had learned in just a few months that if I expected to be successful, I would have to be willing to sacrifice. By then, I was willing to do *anything* to escape the poverty I had known most of my life.

This was clearly my opportunity to *be* somebody. All along I had felt that I was dumb and couldn't do anything in the business world because I was relatively uneducated. But I found that success in *this* business was based not on the past, but on an individual's drive and achievement. I was willing to take the "no's" to get the "yes's" I wanted. And I read many, many books on sales techniques.

I went all out—it was extreme, sure, but it was the only way I knew. For example, the week I was expected to give birth to David, I called on my customers for orders, then Bill and I delivered the orders through the snow the night before I went in to deliver the baby. If people would have known how close the delivery was as I trudged through the snow, they would have thought I was crazy.

But I wanted success so badly, badly enough to keep pushing myself beyond my limits. I wanted to prove myself *to myself*—that I *could* rise above my circumstances.

And the sacrifices were not only on my part—far from it. Bill was right there with me, especially since he saw the business as a tremendous opportunity to grow into himself someday. At night, he drove me to my showings and then took care of Les and David during the time I was inside holding the session.

At first, Bill had our only car, and even after I qualified for the company car, it was several weeks until it arrived. During the coming years, especially if I didn't know the area well, Bill still took me to the showings and picked me up afterwards.

He not only worked during the day, but took care of the children so patiently—feeding, diapering, wiping away those "I want my mama" tears. Our entire family had to pay the price for success. Their sacrifices drove me even harder to go beyond my limitations.

After I qualified for the car, I found out one morning at our studio meeting that Mr. Gochneaur was starting an Executive Club that would consist of the top fifteen managers in the entire company. Even as I sat in the meeting, I seethed with excitement as I made up my mind (ludicrous as it might have seemed at the time) to be one of those top fifteen.

When it came time for the grand finale at the annual convention that year—the "Royal Road to Riches"—I was both shocked and thrilled to see yet another dream come true. I had been named a member of the prestigious Executive Club! I was indeed one of the top fifteen managers in the nation!

I went back home more enthused than ever. I won recruiting contests and booking contests—prizes, furs, and diamonds. Nothing could stop me. I held an average of five shows a week while spending hours on the telephone (yes, we finally did get one!) selling repeat business and interviewing prospective consultants. When Bill wasn't available, I would hire a babysitter to watch Les and David, but otherwise I refused to spend any money that I didn't absolutely have to. Bill and I had previously decided that, as soon as possible, he would join me in the business. Our ultimate goal was to have our own training and distribution center like Marge and Howard Schultz. We lived on what Bill made in his sales job and banked everything I made—determined that one day we would go for our share of the "big money."

Even as Bill and I walked down the "Royal Road to Riches" the first time, I was exploding inside. I loved it! I had found something I could do and do it well. At that moment, I pictured in my mind the ultimate Fashion Two-Twenty goal—to be the number one distributor in the world!

And from that moment on, I thought about my goal from the moment I woke up until my head plopped (maybe collapsed is a better word!) on my pillow at night. It was as if I was driven by an uncontrollable force, but I liked where I was being driven—to the top!

I realized how important it was to *think success*. Wise men and prophets throughout history have disagreed on nearly every major philosophical thought, but on this point all great teachers have agreed—*we are what we think about*.

King Solomon wrote: "As a man thinks in his heart, so is he."

Marcus Aurelius mused, "A man's life is what his thoughts make of it."

Ralph Waldo Emerson said this—"A man is what he thinks about all day long."

Clearly my goal—my impossible dream—was to become the top distributor in my industry. All I had to do was work, work, work! I had to learn to dwell on the positive things rather than the unpleasant, negative, and petty things that anyone encounters in any field.

In my mind, I could see myself holding Bill's arm as we walked down the "Royal Road to Riches" to receive the uppermost award—the highest echelon in our business. Getting our own studio and training center was just part of the dream.

Chapter Twelve

The Dream Becomes A Nightmare

Something was happening to me.

I had just received my second company car, a 1968 Chevrolet Impala. I had sponsored—directly or indirectly—eleven managers, two of whom had also received company cars. Together my managers and I had sponsored 150 consultants, all of whom I trained at different meetings in my home. Bill was doing so well in his sales position that we had finally purchased our own home in Greensboro.

But soon after I won the Executive Club status at the last International Convention, I began to notice that something was wrong. I was feeling so weak. And the weakness didn't go away.

Then one morning I woke up sick—totally nauseous. It was that old familiar queasiness. Sure enough, when I went to see my doctor, another rabbit died! The baby was due on our ninth wedding anniversary.

So, that was it! Still, I was bound and determined that I wasn't going to let anything keep me from the goals I had made for myself. I had made my plans and nothing (not even an unborn infant) was going to stop me.

I kept working—weak or not. Every morning, I went through the ritual of being sick, then forced myself to get dressed and get busy. By lunch time, I had worked the telephone all morning making appointments and following up on repeat sales. Afternoons and evenings were spent either training new consultants or holding showings. By late night, I had completed my records and receipt slips in time to fall into bed.

When I could, I'd sandwich time in for Bill and the boys. We would try to do special things— picnics, outings, impromptu parties. For the most part, though, there was little time for them—I had to reach my goals. There would have to be time for them later in my life—after I had seen my impossible dreams fulfilled.

About six months before that third baby was born, I started getting very, very sick. I began having heart palpitations. I would wake up in the morning with tremors so bad that I couldn't hold anything steady.

I had been weak off and on since David had been born, but nothing like this. I was increasingly afraid that something was wrong, but, with my goals to reach, I kept on going.

Just weeks before the baby was born, Marge and Howard Schultz came to our home and told us that Charlotte, North Carolina, was going to be available as a Fashion Two-Twenty franchise, and that the home office was willing to give Bill and me first option to buy it.

Needless to say, we jumped at the chance! This was the next big rung on our ladder to the top. We had watched our bank account rise, always knowing that it was going to someday buy our own studio and training center. In a moment, we let Marge and Howard know that we were interested. Then, we let the office in Ohio also know our intentions to buy the franchise.

Bill had become the top salesman for People's Life Insurance Company, but he had also realized the greater potential in owning our own business. All along, he had planned to join me in the business when we could get a studio of our own.

In the meantime, my delivery date, which was also Labor Day and our ninth anniversary, came around. So much had happened since those precious moments when Bill and I had stood together—our young hearts beating fast—in the little Baptist church back in West Virginia.

As our anniversary approached, I remember saying to Bill—"Wouldn't it be funny if *I really did* go into labor on Labor Day?"

Sure enough—that's exactly what happened. Becky was born right after midnight—all six, beautiful pounds of her! At last we had our little girl.

The soreness notwithstanding, I had reason to

be the happiest woman in the world. Bill and I were successful. We had a beautiful family, made even more perfect by the addition of our baby girl. We owned cars. We owned our lovely home in Greensboro. We were going to Ohio soon after that to finalize plans to buy our franchise so we could open our own studio. Our families thought we were crazy to leave our business in Greensboro behind to start over in Charlotte, but we wanted the studio, and to get it we had to move to another area. Call it a high-risk gamble, call it faith—we were willing to take the chance to get what we wanted.

Those years in West Virginia seemed so distant. I was on top of my growing, flourishing world. Nothing could stop me now!

But, it didn't take long after Becky's first cries echoed through the delivery room for me to realize that something awful was wrong. I thought at first that it was because the delivery had taken so much out of me, then I thought afterwards that it was the typical "third day blues," but I also knew that something was horribly different this time.

I was sinking down into a deep hole of depression. Before, I could always pull myself out when I felt this happening, but I had a terrible feeling in the pit of my stomach that I wouldn't get out of it this time.

The doctor mentioned the "third day" syndrome when I told him my fears, but his words weren't reassuring at all.

I thought it was because of the hospital, that I would get better when I got home. Bill took Becky and me home when the baby was nine days old. I couldn't go home sooner because of a fever.

The doctor kept telling me that the depression I was feeling would "go away" by itself. I wanted so desperately to believe that what he said was true. I was so glad to go home because Roger Gochneaur, who had replaced his father as the President of Fashion Two-Twenty, was coming to Greensboro to hold a big meeting the same night I was released from the hospital. Bill and the doctors warned me not to go to the meeting, but I felt that I had to go.

There was a reason, of course. The depression scared me. I wanted to get out and get back into the business. That had always worked before. Besides, I had some short *and* long range goals; I sure didn't want to lose momentum.

I knew—as any child does—that once a bicycle is moving, the rider has to keep pedaling to stay up. The biker can coast a few times. But, without a lot of pedaling, the bike will begin wobbling and eventually topple over.

That couldn't happen to me—not with my hard-earned business. I still had too many hills to climb. I had come too far. I already had a chunk of my big dream, and I wasn't stopping for anything.

That night, when I got home from the hospital and went to the big Fashion Two-Twenty meeting, people couldn't see just how weak I was because I was all smiles. I basked in the "I can't believe you've bounced back from the birth so soon!" comments, but inwardly I knew better. I was so jittery with tremors—I just hoped that it didn't look like I had been on a drunken binge or anything. That's how bad I felt. I just wanted to get home.

The next few weeks were even worse. My vision became blurred. I was so weak—it became an effort to walk even a few steps. I was always short of breath, and my heart would palpitate very rapidly. I was nervous, very depressed, very unhappy. An unexplainable fear gripped me, but no one knew it because of the false, happy face I wore.

Inside, I withdrew from everybody. I didn't really want to see anyone. I couldn't stand to be around people. But I didn't stop going as much as I could. I kept dragging myself all over—trying to keep up the facade of a "make it happen" career woman.

Not long after Becky's birth, Bill and I drove to Aurora, Ohio—the Fashion Two-Twenty headquarters—to be interviewed for the franchise in Charlotte.

I was weak—so weak. I had to lean on Bill to walk. My appetite was almost completely gone; I was under a hundred pounds (compared to my 120-plus norm).

Regardless, I kept going, and the interview went without a hitch. We were accepted and paid the company a $10,000 check as a down-payment on the franchise.

Then we started home. I was nearing some kind of a collapse—it was a time of terror and pain. We had left the children with Bill's mother in West Virginia when we went to Ohio, so we had to go back to Charleston to pick up our family. By the time we arrived, however, my mind was far from anticipating seeing my children. I was shivering (though no one else thought it was cold), short of breath, and every little bump on the road seemed like a teeth-gnashing jar to me. I was frantic—I felt like I was dying. Fear choked my heart as if it held it in some monstrous grip.

I asked Bill to take me to the emergency room at the Charleston hospital. There I was placed in a wheelchair, and they wheeled me through the Thomas Memorial Hospital Emergency Room—a burnt-out, collapsing, wasted wreck.

After my initial examination by the on-duty doctor, the physician went outside the room and talked to Bill. Bill explained what I had gone through during the past few weeks, so the doctor—instead of administering further tests—just told Bill that I was a high-strung girl: "She's just reacting to all that's been going on—the baby, the business venture; that's all! Get her home and rested up, and she'll be as good as new."

I couldn't believe that the doctor couldn't see that I was deathly ill. I knew that it was more than what they said—more than some psychosomatic symptoms—I could have handled that.

So they bundled me up, and Bill took me and the children on home to Greensboro.

Life had to go on, sickness or not. We had to move to Charlotte as soon as possible. We had to sell our house. We had to get Les ready to change schools.

I'm afraid that I wasn't much help during this time. By mid-October, I had to be admitted to the hospital again—this time Moses Cone Hospital in Greensboro. The doctors ran more tests, but still found no reason for my illness. It got more puzzling all the time—more for me than for the doctors.

And it was while I was a patient in Moses Cone that I began to believe that I was going to die. Bill had taken the children back to his mother's in West Virginia. One entire day I lay thinking of my life, my precious little children that I would never get to see again, my husband that had been so patient, our fledgling business. It all seemed so far away—all my dreams, all my hopes, all my plans.

I was so weak—weaker than I could get anyone to believe—and I was being swallowed up in a deep, dark pit. I knew I was dying. I figured that Bill and the doctors knew more than they were telling me, and that they were afraid to tell me for fear that I would give up completely. Was it some terminal illness?

By the time Bill came in that evening, I begged him to call the home office and ask them to return the

$10,000 we had given them—"You'll need it when I'm gone—please move back to West Virginia where our parents can help take care of our babies."

I was weeping uncontrollably. "Please, just bring me our big picture album. I want to see our babies' faces one last time before I die."

Of course, Bill did neither. I think he believed that if he did bring in the pictures, I really would give up.

Bill tried to spend as much time with me as possible, but he also had to get everything ready to leave for Charlotte.

Meanwhile, I spent my time weeping—wondering what would happen next. I had no resiliency or "bounce-back" left in me at all. It was all so unlike me. After a few days of this horrible nightmare, my doctor came in, sat on the bedside, crinkled a smile, patted me on the leg, and chatted about my "spastic splenic colisticitis" that was brought on by so much stress. He gave me a prescription for librium and libriacs, and cracked—"Well, young lady, you're going home tomorrow!"

I was totally nonplussed. Of course I wanted to go home, but his whole manner, the trite diagnosis, had me in a turmoil. I knew there was more wrong with me than merely a spastic colon and spleen. Paranoid or not, I was more positive than ever that I *did* have a terminal illness. Going home so suddenly obviously seemed to be the last step of my personal, hideous journey into the unknown. My mind was so groggy that I couldn't begin to comprehend it all; I just kept weeping uncontrollably.

After the move to Charlotte, I lay in the dark bedroom—I couldn't stand light or sound. Bill had packed for the movers all by himself.

I was beyond doing anything. All I wanted to do was sleep. There was no more "take charge" career woman facade. I had collapsed. I just couldn't cope with life anymore. All I wanted to do was escape.

I made no more pretenses. I don't know how Bill stood it—I became a total recluse in the darkness and quiet of my room. I laid in bed day after day. The blinds were closed. The least bit of sound pounded in my ears, and even a glimmer of light stunned my eyes.

For the girl who had lived beauty and cosmetics for so many years, I suddenly became the extreme opposite. I couldn't stand looking in the mirror—my hair was straggly, my fingernails became jagged, and my skin was swarthy and yellow-looking. I looked more like an old hag than a beauty queen. My hair had fallen out by the handfuls; I had bald places the size of quarters, nickels, and dimes.

Bill hoped that I would "snap out of it" like the doctors said I would. He tried to help me, but I couldn't respond without weeping and screaming. He was so patient and kind—so caring for the children and me. He had gone back to Charleston and brought the children home, and he was caring for them all by himself.

Weeks passed. Months passed. I ate little, drank less. My joints were so dehydrated that I cried out in pain every time I had to change positions. My whole body was hurting, even lying in bed.

I was in a hole. It was a deep, dark pit. It seemed like I would never get out. I started imagining that someone was in my closet, under my bed, or looking through the cracks of the drawn drapes.

If only someone would have been able to say, "Wilda, there's hope." But no one said that. Everyone just wanted me to *snap out of it*—but I couldn't do it this time. I was being totally consumed by this horrible fear. I knew that I really would die unless someone helped me.

I felt my life trying to leave my body several times. I never went as far as the "out of the body" experiences that many people have talked about, but each time I would have to fight to keep my spirit from leaving. I knew that if I didn't get some help—I could not hold on any longer. I was losing the fight.

I clung to the glimmering hope that there was more for me to do yet. I wanted to see my children grow and mature. I wanted to see my dreams fulfilled.

My impossible dream had changed. I didn't care about anything but getting out of this black pit. I was like a swimmer on the ocean—going down for the last time, gasping for breath as I sank to the bottom. Somehow all of my thrashing and fighting just seemed to push me deeper.

I only wanted to get out, but I just didn't know how.

Chapter Thirteen

Light . . . and Hope

Bill didn't know what to do with me anymore. He gave me so much understanding and even hired a housekeeper whom we called "Grandma." But it looked like the end of life as we had known it.

Then, when I was at my lowest, a dear friend, Claire, sent me a copy of *Good News For Modern Man*, a modern translation of the New Testament. I was lying in that dark, morgue-like bedroom, grasping for anything I thought would help me out of that deep, dark hole.

I would lie in my bed in the semi-darkness and read a page or two of this *Good News*. I had never really understood the Bible that well, so I was surprised to find that I could understand this modern-language version. It was so different from the "begats," "thees," and "thous" in the King James Version.

I read it in short intervals; then had to close my eyes for a while. It was almost like solitary confinement since I couldn't stand any sounds around me yet, and "Grandma" kept the children busy. So I had nothing to do except read the words in the book—I kept it propped up on a pillow:

"So then, as the Holy Spirit says: 'If you hear God's voice today, do not be stubborn, as your ancestors were when they rebelled against God, as they were that day in the desert when they put Him to the test . . .'

"Be careful that no one among you has a heart so evil and unbelieving that he will turn away from the living God. Instead, in order that none of you be deceived by sin and become stubborn, you must help one another everyday. . . . For we are all partners with Christ if we hold firmly to the end the confidence we had at the beginning" (Hebrews 3:7-8, 12-14).

The other verses that meant a lot to me were in the last Epistle from the dear, elderly apostle John:

" . . . Now the message that we have heard from His Son and announce is this: God is light, and there is no darkness at all in Him. If, then, we say that we have fellowship with Him, yet at the same time live in the darkness, we are lying both in our words and in our actions. But if we live in the light, just as He is in the light, then we have fellowship with one another, and the blood of Jesus, His Son, makes us clean from every sin.

"If we say that we have no sin, we deceive ourselves, and there is no truth in us. But if we confess our sins to God, we can trust Him, for He does what is right—He will forgive us of our sins and make us clean from all our wrongdoing" (1 John 1:5-9).

In three months, I had read the New Testament

101

all the way through. I remember the moment when I finished that *Good News For Modern Man*. I closed it and looked up at the ceiling to reflect about what I had read. Suddenly, I began thinking about the years since childhood.

Scenes flashed through my mind—the night Daddy came back from the revival, changed forever. I remembered the clean feeling I had when I, too, accepted Jesus into my heart. It was the same feeling that I had when I deliberately chose God's way as a teenager, especially during the wild Hollywood weeks.

So when had it all changed? How had I been transformed from a freshly-scrubbed teenager who loved Jesus into a witch-looking, burnt-out, young woman who couldn't exist except in her darkened, soundless bedroom? How had I gone from a happy bride to a haglike skeleton with no appetite or strength? And how had I stumbled into this death-pit? Was it because God no longer cared about me—the non-religious, cocktail-partying, "take charge" woman? Or was it that God couldn't love me? I had always had a problem with that; it's hard for an unloved child to get past those scars. Just the thoughts of my childhood made me start crying.

I took some time that day to get past all the questions, but finally I looked up at the shadows on the ceiling and began talking outloud—weeping and praying:

"God, I know You are there. And I know that

You *do* love me—this book has reminded me of that.

"God, I don't want to die! Please let me get out of this hole. Help me—please!

"And God—if You raise me up—if You let me raise my children—then I'll serve You the rest of my life."

Now, maybe it wasn't a great theological petition, but there comes a time when "theology" goes out the window and *"Help"* is the only cry left. Sometimes the most powerful prayers are sobs rather than pious phrases.

I was at that *"Help"* stage. I had held on for so long, and at last I let go and let myself drop into God's hands.

For a woman who had been such an achiever, to acknowledge God's overpowering hand was no small feat. But what else could I do when faced with the blackness, eeriness, and endlessness of a slimy pit? Crying to God and saying "help" was all I had left.

Shortly after that prayer, my first miracle occurred.

One day an old friend who had recently moved to Charlotte from Greensboro came over to see me. Gloria wasn't prepared for what she saw. She took one long look at me, her face grimacing like she had seen a ghost. "Wilda Sue," she exclaimed, "what in the world is wrong with you? You look positively awful!"

"I don't know. The doctors have checked me,"

I rasped. "I've been sick for a year, but I've only been this bad for three or four months."

She immediately demanded that I get out of bed, then went and called her doctor—a specialist.

Dr. Johnson (not his real name), I found out, was more than just a dispenser of drugs and trite prognoses. He was deeply committed to curing the problem, not just dealing with the symptoms.

Dr. Johnson examined me and took blood samples. Shortly after he finished and determined the diagnosis, he came back into the room where I sat. "Mrs. Marple," he intoned, "you're a very sick girl. You've got infectious mononucleosis. Your liver and spleen are swollen which is caused by the infection." He continued listing things wrong with me. One of the even greater problems was that I had swollen and infected glands in several different parts of my body.

Then the doctor said, "We can help you though; we're going to get you started in regaining your strength and getting over those vitamin deficiencies."

I started crying, but not the uncontrollable weeping I had experienced all the previous months. These were tears of joy because it looked like someone was going to finally help me.

I had almost given up hope. Now I was being offered at least a glimmer. A specialist was saying what I had believed for so long—that I wasn't crazy, that I did have something medically wrong, and that drugs alone wouldn't cure me. In my heart I knew that this help had come as a direct result of my prayer. I could hardly wait to share it with Bill.

The doctor started me on a crash program of antibiotics and Vitamin B shots, but he warned me that it would be a slow process. It would take about a year to get over my serious case of mononucleosis.

My answers to prayer weren't finished yet.

Shortly after that first visit, I was given the glucose tolerance test, and they discovered, on top of the mononucleosis, that I also had very low blood sugar, or hypoglycemia. The doctor said that I had probably suffered from it for years. It was the low blood sugar that had caused those horrible heart palpitations, tremors, and nausea.

In reading about hypoglycemia, I discovered what I should eat and how often I should eat—small meals six times a day. Even with this new discovery, it was some time before my weakness and tremors were finally gone.

At least . . . it was a beginning.

The darkness was still there, and despite the help the medicine and vitamins had been, I was still extremely weak. At times, the deep, dark pit seemed just as real and looming as before, but deep down I knew that there was finally hope.

I was so thankful for all that the doctor had begun to do for me, and that he understood some of my physical problems. But I knew that I needed more than anything the medical world had to offer me to get out this time.

In the end, it was that *prayer*, my cry for help from deep within my spirit, that brought me light and hope for the climb back.

Chapter Fourteen

Nothing Stands in the Way

Slowly but surely, I began to notice a change. It was as though life was coming back into my body.

I began to care about how I looked. For months I hadn't bothered to take care of myself—my fingernails, my hair, my face. I began looking in the mirror again for the first time in a long time. I began to notice that the slightest sounds were no longer throbbing in my ears as before. I could even stand daylight. I started to regain my appetite. Slowly, at first, I began getting out of my bed for longer periods.

I wanted to live again, to care for my husband and children, to someday work again. I had tasted death; now I wanted to relish every moment of life.

And I had so much catching up to do. It was early 1969, and I had been sick for nearly a year. It had been seven months since I had worked at all.

During that year, I had almost totally neglected Bill and the children. Poor Becky, she had cried so much in her crib—she hardly knew who her

Mommy was.

Bill would sometimes bring my little baby girl into my darkened room and lay her beside me, but inevitably he would soon have to take her back into another part of the house. I couldn't stand any noise. Any sound, especially her shrill cries, was like thunder in my ears.

Becky, even in her infancy, sensed that something was wrong. Ever since we had come home from the hospital, I had never held her much or spent a lot of time with her. I had been too far down in the black hole to even be aware of her needs.

So—after I began getting better—Becky and I started acquainting ourselves. Nobody will ever know the agony I went through those many months. I was totally guilt-ridden at not being able to cope with life, at neglecting my little baby, at not being able to cuddle or play with Les and David. They needed those things for their own normal growth and emotional stability. I just didn't have anything left to give.

David and Les were little troupers, for sure, but the dark period had also taken its toll on them. Birthdays, Thanksgiving, Christmas—all the special days of 1968—had passed without frolic or festivities.

Somehow Bill accomplished the impossible—caring for a quizzically, critically ill wife and keeping his children clothed and fed—all while moving to a different city and trying to find a building to open our new studio in at the same time.

How Bill did it with so much gentleness and patience—I'll never know. But he became more precious to me daily.

Our entire household went through the most indescribably miserable period any family could ever know. It was like some evil, monstrous hand had shrouded our home for nearly a year.

Finally, at last, the stench of death was gone!

One of the rays of sunshine during those dark days had been the hiring of "Grandma" to be our housekeeper. She came to us just as I was beginning to see a flicker of light at the end of the tunnel.

Her name was Willie Mae Moore, but she asked us to call her "Grandma." Bill knew that I was still very sick and that I would need help during my recuperation period.

He was right. Grandma helped . . .and helped. She was a big, white, Southern woman who was the epitome of the name she had asked us to call her. She cooked meals fit for Southern aristocracy, and she immediately took the kids to her heart. We all loved her—how we loved her.

She fixed beautiful, appetizing feasts and coaxed me to eat. She literally nursed me back to health. "Wilda, hon," she would say, "eat this, and it will make you strong again."

She quickly became part of our family. She had previously lived with one of her sons and his family since her husband had died of a heart attack during the mid-sixties.

Life since her husband's death had been miserable. She told us that there had been a great deal of strife and fighting where she had been staying. Finally, when she couldn't take it any longer, she boarded a Greyhound Bus. She returned on that bus to Charlotte where she and her late husband had spent so many happy years.

When she came to us, she was downtrodden and unkempt. As I began to get better, I helped her learn to apply cosmetics. Then she got her hair fixed. She started looking pretty, so she felt pretty. I guess in some ways we were a godsend to her, too.

And we certainly knew just how much we needed her. For Bill, Grandma was a freedom-giver. He was finally able to get out and get something going in the business. Grandma literally took over the house—she did everything: the cooking, the cleaning, wiping dirty noses, hugging hurt children, and playing games with them, too.

For the kids, Grandma meant spices and cookies and a tender shoulder to cry on. She also was a strict disciplinarian—as David soon found out. He was such an all-boy boy, and one day he threw a little plastic chair down the steps. Well, that didn't set well with Grandma at all, so she promptly marched the tow-headed three-year-old down the stairs and made him drag the chair back up. He, like Les, learned a well-earned lesson: Grandma was no pushover.

For me, Grandma gave me the added incentive and liberty of trying to get back out into the business world. I was still taking it easy—Bill *and* Dr. Johnson saw to that—but I knew that I couldn't take the prescribed year to recuperate. I had to make up for so much lost time. Like it or not, whether I felt well or not, we had invested almost every penny we had into the Charlotte franchise, so I had to jump back into the "frying pan."

On March 17, 1969—a few months after I began my long road to recovery—we had the Grand Opening of our studio. It was the culmination of so many hard-fought dreams.

The studio hadn't come without struggles and efforts and sacrifices. It meant that on Les' first day of school, I was out holding a morning demonstration. It meant that most of our clothing had been bought at K-Mart bargain racks. It meant that we had forgone luxuries like air-conditioning and color TV's. We had lived in small, thrifty houses, even when we could have afforded much better.

I had been blind to anything else but being successful in the business. I ignored the warnings when my body told me to relax and rest more. I felt that I was paving a way for happiness for our family—someday later we could enjoy that happiness. But for that time, we had to work!

I had wrecked my health, but I had kept my eyes on the goal—kept pressing on. So the Grand Opening of the Charlotte studio (once a furniture warehouse) meant a giant step.

For the first time, Bill and I were actually running *our* business. We made a great team—even if I was a little skeptical at turning over so much of it to Bill. I had been used to doing everything—the books, the ordering, training new consultants—everything.

Bill was quiet and yet aggressive—a super salesman; he brought a wealth of sales principles to share with our growing number of consultants. Also, he had a keen mind for business organization—something sorely needed as the distribution volume increased dramatically during the coming months and years.

When it came time to form our own corporation, Bill was named president and I was vice-president. We each owned an equal amount of stock in the corporation. Bill did the preliminary interviews when we hired new consultants—telling the women about the company and the tremendous financial opportunities. Then, I would tell them about the products, give sample demonstrations, and discuss the responsibilities. Bill had the final decision about approving a prospective consultant; then I would begin the training sessions in earnest. For the training program, we approved nearly everyone who wanted the opportunity because we kept remembering where we had come from and all the reasons why I shouldn't have succeeded in the business.

But once the training actually began, Bill and I were pretty strict. We knew that quitters would never make it in the business, so we tried to screen out the people who didn't seem willing to make the needed sacrifices. Quitters just wasted our time, and we had so much that we wanted to do in the little time that we had.

It was a healthy relationship for us as business partners and marriage partners. We became best friends. I had come out of that deep, dark hole. With the vitamins I had started taking, and with so many of my physical problems finally gone (or at least *going*), I was not depressed and continually run-down like I had been before. Obviously Bill preferred the new *me* to that ill woman he had been dragging along during the past year. We were getting along better than we had gotten along in our lives. Moreover, we were now united more than ever in our quest for that top niche in the world of Fashion Two-Twenty.

The first month—April, 1969—after opening the Charlotte studio, we did $13,000 volume, we trained seven new consultants, and we had already reached out to open a new studio in Fayetteville, North Carolina, which was about 150 miles from Charlotte.

Shortly afterward, we sponsored another studio in Gaston County—just west of Charlotte. During 1969 and 1970, we continued buying franchises and opening studios. By 1971 we had bought the territory for all of eastern Tennessee and western North Carolina. We also moved our headquarters to an "uptown" area of Charlotte.

We began winning many contests. One of the first was a recruiting contest to anyone who could sign and train fifty new consultants within two months. We made a commitment—made up our minds that we were going to do it—and began working day and night. At the end of the two months, we had recruited sixty-seven women, and I had won an incredibly rich-looking, autumn-haze mink cape with a Russian sable collar, tailored just for me; a label inside read "*Made especially for Wilda Sue Marple.*"

Also during August, 1971, we bought our first Charlotte home. We had rented for three years since our arrival in the Queen City, but felt that we could finally indulge and enjoy some of the rewards for our hard work—a six-bedroom, three-bath house in the posh southeast section of Charlotte.

We ordered new furniture for the first time since our early years of marriage—some specially made, hand-carved, and custom-painted.

For Becky's third birthday, we went shopping for an elegant white and gold French Provential bedroom suite to match her white, pink, and orchid room.

The boys likewise had rooms customized to suit their own tastes.

At times, I would walk through the house after everyone had gone to sleep and have to pinch myself to see if I was dreaming. I couldn't help thinking back to the time when I was a skinny little girl whose entire house had less rooms than I now had for bedrooms. I would wander into the spicy-smelling, shiny new kitchen and see nearly forgotten images of us little kids foraging through the woods—looking for mulberries and hazel nuts.

But that was so far away. Our business was growing and prospering. We were beginning to realize profits and were making more money than we had ever dreamed possible.

And the dream—the impossible dream to climb to the top of the entire world of Fashion Two-Twenty—was nearing our growing grasp. That one thing was our goal—and nothing could stand in our way to reach it.

Chapter Fifteen

Dream Chasers

With our determination to reach the top, work was very serious. But as we prospered, the humorous moments grew. Some of our craziest times were with Grandma.

Grandma had a habit of throwing away every last piece of loose paper she saw lying around. One morning I was getting ready to leave the house and go to work; I rushed past the countertop to get my appointment book where I always laid it at night after holding a show. But it wasn't there. Panic! Suddenly it hit me that Grandma had mistakenly thrown it in the trash can. Just as I was figuring out what happened, I heard the garbage truck out in the street.

I had never raised my voice to Grandma, but I let the questions fly fast and furiously as I anxiously tried to see if she could remember where my appointment book was.

She couldn't; so, in desperation, I ran outside past our just-emptied trash cans and down the street to the garbage truck. The sanitation workers must have thought I was a crazy woman (at the moment they wouldn't have been far off!) as I explained my predicament. They had no idea where—in all the steamy, look-a-like bags—my garbage was, so I promptly informed them that I would personally search through all their stinking trash for my appointment book.

What a picture—me, the sophisticated, well-dressed business woman in high heels and shimmering jewelry, climbing up on the truck to pilfer through milk cartons and coffee grounds. I searched frantically for my precious appointment book through every bag. All I could think of was the hundreds and hundreds of dollars worth of showings and appointments. I had no duplicate copy, and there was no possible way for me to remember even a tenth of my schedule.

After scrounging through the mounds of trash as the grinning, puzzled men looked on, I finally had to give up. I just couldn't find it. Hundreds of dollars worth of bookings were in that book somewhere in the truck, and I couldn't find it!

I tried to shake off all the pieces of paper and food scraps hanging on me as I walked back dejectedly to the house. I was determined to give Grandma a blistering piece of my mind for throwing away everything in sight—especially my precious appointment book.

As I trudged up the driveway (hoping that

none of my neighbors had seen my chaotic display!), I happened to glance in my car and spied something familiar lying on the car seat. Right! My appointment book!

Cringe. I was suddenly filled with shame at the way I had acted, accusing Grandma of throwing the book away. I knew I had to "face the music." I went in and tried to tell Grandma. We both cried like babies, then laughed together. Though it was over in just a few hectic moments, it had been the first rift between us.

Bill and I were on our way home that evening with me still living and reliving that horrible morning scene—yelling at Grandma and scrounging through the mass of trash like a wild animal. I felt so sorry for the way I acted. As we passed a shopping center, I remembered how Grandma had cooed over a doll that she had seen in one of the stores. I asked Bill to turn around so that I could go inside to buy it—a beautiful doll dressed in a red velvet coat with an ostrich feather cap. When we got home and I gave it to her, we cried all over again.

Grandma had never had anything like it. All her life she had served people. Her father had died in a railroad accident, and her mother had been so shy that she couldn't even bear to go to town. When Grandma married and left the farm, she still served people—her three children and later her ten grandchildren.

She was getting older now and getting weary

of raising children. She had changed thousands of dirty diapers and had washed a mountain of bottles.

When she came to work for us, she let us know that she would raise Becky and the boys, but no more babies!

Imagine my surprise when I woke up one morning in the summer of 1974 with the old familiar queasiness. It didn't dawn on me that I might be pregnant until the next morning when I woke up with the same sick feeling. I panicked!

The first thing I thought of was all our plans for the future—the goals were nearer than ever. The second thought that exploded in my mind was all the blackness I had experienced before and after Becky had been born.

We were getting ready to start construction on a beautiful chalet in the North Carolina mountains.

We were so busy working and recruiting. Bill and I had already been recognized the previous January as one of the top ten distributors in the world of Fashion Two-Twenty.

I had already informed our closest associates of our firm intentions to be the number one distributors.

Any way I considered it, a baby just didn't fit into our plans. I loved our three children, but I didn't want any more—especially now.

I went to the calendar and counted the days since my last period. Sure enough, I had missed one. I called the doctor—made an appointment. More bad news—another rabbit died!

I went to pieces when the doctor confirmed the pregnancy. I told him all about our plans. I said that I couldn't stand to go through what I went through with Becky. I also knew that I didn't want to have to go—at least for now—without Grandma.

The doctor listened patiently, then mentioned an alternative—abortion. He explained the 1973 abortion decision that had been made by the Supreme Court the year before. I was interested, so I went home and discussed it with Bill.

The discussion didn't last long, though. I knew that I wasn't going through with another pregnancy. Bill was supportive of whichever way I chose to act.

Two days later, we went to the studio in the morning like any other day, but that same morning we left to go to the hospital. Bill went along so that both of us could sign the necessary papers. At the admission desk, I was asked, "Why are you coming in?" I used my most sophisticated, chic voice— "Abortion."

My mind began racing. Until then, I hadn't really thought about the seriousness of the step I was taking—that I was taking a life. They called "it" a fetus, so it seemed so depersonalized, but it was still a life. I pushed out of my mind what God might think about abortion.

God... it had been some time since I had even thought about the God I had promised to "serve all the rest of my life" when He healed me from that horrible, deep pit of despair and mononucleosis five years before in 1969.

The longer I waited in the hospital, the more horrible I felt. Even as the nurse began priming me for "surgery," I knew that what I was doing was tragically wrong. If I had been honest enough with myself to realize that it wasn't "surgery" at all, but the murder of an unborn infant, I would have undoubtedly walked out as determined as I walked in. But I had already passed the point of no return.

It all happened so fast; I had tried to keep from thinking about what I was doing. In a short time, I was anesthetized. Then I woke up, and it was all over. I was no longer pregnant.

But I wasn't as carefree as I thought I would be. As Bill took me home that afternoon, I was quiet—trying to sort out my thoughts without really thinking about what had happened in the previous hours.

I didn't remember hearing much talk about abortion before this—maybe it was just that I didn't listen—but from that point on it seemed like everything I saw or heard had that word in it—abortion. I didn't want to be reminded, but there it was on everything—billboards, radio, newspaper.

One day I watched a TV program. Sure enough, the subject suddenly turned to abortion. There, in living, horrible color, were scenes of babies after they had been aborted—little hands, feet, ears, eyes—all whole but without the chance to ever develop.

Until then, I had honestly thought that the fetal period was just a starting stage for a human, that the little embryo was a "thing." But faced with the facts, I had to admit that I was indeed a murderer. I had been responsible for killing my unborn baby just as much as if I had paid an assassin to murder Les, David, or Becky.

Up until that time, I had never considered myself much of a sinner. I had always been a good girl. I had never been in any trouble as a child, never committed fornication or adultery as a young woman, never taken drugs—the things people generally consider "bad" sins.

But when I saw that program on television, I realized that I was a murderer—a horrible sin. I wondered if God could ever forgive me. Had I committed the unforgivable sin? I realized I was as guilty of murder as a convicted killer languishing behind bars. Sure, people had put the stamp of public approval on abortion, but I could see the little, unformed babies piled up on the television picture.

Guilt became a very real part of my life. I couldn't shake it off. My doctor prescribed valium to deaden the pain and guilt so that I could get to sleep.

With great determination, I tried crowding out such thoughts. I was too busy reaching my dreams.

I was also too busy picking out the carpet, lights, and paneling for our mountain chalet. Every weekend, we'd pile the kids in the station wagon and head for the mountains. Until the chalet was finished, we stayed in the nearby Wolf Laurel Inn and partied all weekend—dances, games, barbeques.

It was a fast life—a merry-go-round. There were times I longed to get off. I was getting tired of the rat race. I was constantly fighting my old nemesis—low blood sugar. And now I was also fighting a deep-seated case of guilt over the abortion.

It would have helped if Bill and I would have talked about the abortion, but we never did. I just assumed that he never wanted to discuss it again; likewise, he thought that my silence about the abortion meant that I didn't want to think about it anymore.

So on we went—hurting, but busy—dream-chasers getting close to "paydirt."

Chapter Sixteen

A Banner Year

The year 1975 was definitely a banner year for the Marples. Our business stretched by this time from the Piedmont area of North Carolina all the way through the mountains of Tennessee—pretty good for a business that had started ten years before with just a $31.50 initial investment!

The founder of Fashion Two-Twenty, Mr. V. G. Gochneaur, was impressed enough to ask Bill and me to consider heading the company in England. But we decided against moving—we didn't want to leave behind the opportunities we had going.

One painful time that year was when Grandma decided to leave us. We saw that she was having an increasingly hard time coping with the children. She was getting older and forgetful, and was suffering from hardening of the arteries. One of her sons wanted her to come and live with his family—so finally, we all decided that it would be best if she did go. To my surprise, it opened up a whole new world for me.

The day Grandma left, I spent the entire day at home. I had a few hours to think, and suddenly it hit me that, for the first time in six years, the responsibility of being a mother was on me—cooking, washing, helping with homework, bandaging scraped knees. It was a little frightening, but I also felt a sense of excitement that I had never felt before as I waited for the schoolbus to bring my children home.

That was the beginning of a new schedule for me. I began enjoying being a mother. I would go to work at 9 a.m. after the children left, then rush home before the schoolbus arrived in the afternoon.

Of course, there were moments of painful aching for Grandma—after all, she had lived with us for six years. We all missed her, especially Becky. We looked forward to Grandma's occasional weekend visits.

All of that led up to a special morning in May. I had gotten the children off to school, then took a cup of coffee into the den—"Ah, what a life of leisure!" Even a few hours off a day seemed almost frivolous compared to my non-stop, ten-year Spartan existence.

I flipped the TV on. What I saw was some kind of talk show, but I could tell that it was different from the usual Mike Douglas/Merv Griffin kind.

I heard a man talk about some of the things he had gone through, then he started talking about Jesus Christ. "On a TV talk show?" I thought.

He shared how God loved us so much that He gave His only Son to die for our sins—that no matter what we had done or where we had gone, God *would* forgive us.

I had heard it all before, but as he talked, my heart raced with excitement. "Could God ever forgive me for taking a little baby's life before it had a chance to be born?" I had wandered so far away from God that I had scarcely thought of Him during the past years.

Then the man said something else that pierced my heart: "Everybody has a god—there is a throne in every home. Sometimes it's the wife, the husband, the children, or some materialistic thing." It was true for me. I knew that God had not been on the throne of my life—being a success and making lots of money had always been *number one*.

The man then invited people to pray with him. I knew that I had made a mess of my life—that the merry-go-round I was on wasn't fulfilling me anymore. I was nearing the top, yet I wasn't any happier than I was before. I kept reaching and reaching, yet I had no peace.

I didn't pray with the TV host that day, but I had to admit that I wanted to. The program made me feel refreshed and happy. I was like a little, wilted flower in the desert that had just been watered in a rain shower.

Whatever it was—whatever I felt during the television program—it was great. I felt wonderful.

It was like life was being poured into my limbs. I had tried to keep praying and reading my Bible at different times in my life, especially after God brought me out of that deep, dark pit of depression and illness. But it always seemed like my busy schedule didn't leave much time for God.

Now, I couldn't wait to find another excuse to stay home during the morning and watch that program again. Several days later, I did stay home. I rushed around making sure that all my housework was completed so I would be free to watch the show again.

I tried to be more perceptive this time and less awestruck at a Christian talk show. I realized more than ever that they had something I didn't have. I knew it wasn't a magnetic personality or intriguing charm—people considered me vivacious, pretty, and bubbly, but I knew that I had to wear lots of masks to be that way.

These people sang and talked unashamedly about Jesus.

As the program continued, I became really involved in what they were saying—weeping some, laughing often. For the first time in my life, I began to realize what "there is more" meant—they were talking about a special walk with God. They were describing a joy-filled life.

Even as these thoughts raced through my mind, I began seeing the word *"Abortion! Abortion!"* The hateful word hung over me like a gloomy mental shroud. I was reminded that I had murdered an unborn infant. How could I ever expect *anything* from God after committing murder, much less His love?

Then the man on the TV program spoke, his voice cutting through the questions in my mind. He said, "Would you like to ask God to forgive you of your sins and ask Him to *wipe your slate clean?* Would you like Him to never remember your sins again—just like He promised in His Word? If you do, just ask Him right where you are."

Without a moment's hesitation, I slipped silently to my knees and blurted out a makeshift prayer. I don't remember exactly what I said, but it was some time before I got up from my knees. My eyes were red and swollen, but my heart no longer had a steel clamp encasing it. I could actually feel God's presence in the room.

It was like a flashbulb had gone off in my heart. I realized how far I had slipped away from God— even after the dark and desperate times when I had promised to serve Him forever. I knew that I didn't look or act like the Christian I claimed to be.

I had lived on dreams, especially my Fashion Two-Twenty "impossible dream" for so many years, but I had lived without any real joy and strength.

Obviously *things* could not bring joy; neither could fulfilled material dreams. I had received more than my share of both—but still had no joy.

Could it be like they had said on the TV program, "the joy of the Lord is my strength"?

All I know is that I walked on air for the next few days. I wanted to tell Bill, but I wasn't sure how he would react, so I waited for the appropriate time.

I found that the same program came on at night, so I turned on the program one evening while Bill was sitting in the den. I waited several moments for his reaction, but I wasn't ready for what happened. Bill had obviously heard of the program before; he walked over and snapped the TV set off. He was furious!

"I can't stand to look at that man," he clipped, "much less have to sit and listen to his voice!"

It really took me by surprise. I was hoping that he would like it—that he would be as touched by what they were saying as I had been. My initial shock turned to sobs. Rather than trying to explain something so precious to me, I went into our bedroom.

Several evenings later, I made up my mind to talk to Bill about my new commitment to God, and why I liked the Christian TV program. The moment finally came when I could share it with him:

"Bill, the reason that show on television means so much to me is that I've realized through watching it a few times how far away from God I've been—how much more there is to life than just chasing dreams. And I've turned my life, my sins, my dreams, even the abortion that we've never talked about—I've surrendered all of it to the Lord."

There, I'd said it. I waited for Bill's reaction. Again, I was shocked.

"That's funny," he grinned, "because after you and the kids went to bed the other night, I watched the program, and I've recommitted my life to the Lord, too! I was waiting for the right time to tell you."

God certainly works in mysterious ways. Soon He was working in other ways. Bill said, "Wilda, I think we ought to start going to church again."

Our children had been to church very little, especially David and Becky. They didn't mind going; in fact, during a revival in the local church where we started to attend, all three children accepted Jesus and were water baptized. All of us joined the church, fully meaning to become faithful members.

Frankly, we still got more out of watching the Christian television program, but we knew that we needed to be involved in a local church as well. So we went, and we sat—trying to get something out of the music and sermons.

Within a few months, we began realizing that the few people who had that "something special" like we had seen on the TV program were leaving the church, one by one.

One night as we watched the TV program, a very interesting guest shared his personal testimony and all of the marvelous things that God had done in his life. Then he began to talk about something called "the baptism of the Holy Spirit."

Now, I had been baptized in the Elk River when I was fifteen years old, but this was obviously something different—something I had never heard about. I wondered if the "something special" I was looking for was related to this strange "baptism" they talked about.

I wanted to find out more about this "baptism of the Holy Spirit," but no one that I knew seemed to know anything about it. The church that we were attending—like my childhood church—believed that a person "got it all" when he or she accepted the Lord. I was beginning to see that there was a major difference on the teaching of the subject between the Christian TV program and our church.

Why then, I wondered, did the people who believed in that mysterious "baptism of the Holy Spirit" seem so filled with joy, while the people who thought that a person "got it all at salvation" often seemed dry, lifeless, or ritualistic?

So many questions! I searched what Scriptures I heard on TV. So many things, dreams, and plans had crowded the blessings of God out of my life. I had so much—more than most. I had worked hard to see all my dreams fulfilled, but my spirit and soul were hungry for joy. Prayer and Bible reading were becoming part of my daily regimen. I knew that I was born again and forgiven of all my sins, including the abortion. But, as I searched my new *Living*

Bible, I realized more than ever that something was missing. I wanted the power to actually live the Christian life the way my Savior wanted me to. *That* was becoming a top priority.

An evangelist came to the Charlotte Coliseum for an area-wide crusade supported by many churches, including the one we attended. We went. The place was packed. I was naturally shocked when this well-known preacher began denouncing the very Christian TV program that our family had been so blessed by, but I tried to handle that—after all, a lot of people didn't like the personalities or different types of music. I felt sorry for those who didn't like the program, but I felt that they certainly had a right to their personal opinion. I *was* dubious about this evangelist using the pulpit to denounce another Christian work.

Soon I found that this preacher was just getting started. He moved on to a real shocker—"This so-called baptism of the Holy Spirit, especially with all the overemphasis on 'tongue-talking' is clearly wrong," I heard him say. "After the last apostle died, the power to pass on miracle-working abilities to someone else ceased. This healing and working of miracles that the first century apostles and disciples performed was because there was no written record of Jesus' power. That special power was given only then for the New Testament record. It was needed then, but now we have the completed Scriptures."

That evangelist went on to say, "In other

words, the Bible says that when John the Beloved finished writing the last words of the Book of Revelation on the Isle of Patmos, there was no need for the Word of God to be confirmed further with signs and wonders. The record was complete."

Further, he described in glowing detail the fact that everything we need was right there in the Word of God. As a result, these so-called "miracles" and "the baptism of the Holy Spirit," and "speaking in tongues" had to be from the devil—or at best from peoples' own imaginations.

I felt sick. I was crying on the inside as we left that night. Our family was strangely silent as we drove home.

As soon as I could, I got by myself and began praying—"God, I really thought there was *more*, that there was a fresh, deeper walk available. They've been saying it on TV, but now this preacher says 'No!' Which one is right?"

I had no thundering answer, but I promised the Lord and myself that I would start searching until I did find the truth. I knew that the Bible was right (both the TV people and the Coliseum preacher agreed on that), so I figured that the Bible would show me which position was right.

I decided to find the answers for myself. I wanted the truth—not just a lot of human interpretations. And since I wasn't going to settle for anyone else's word on the matter, I knew I would have to search the Bible until I found the answers. I was certainly willing to dig for something that important.

During the next weeks and months, I really started to search the Word of God. I was continually praying, "Lord, please show me if this baptism of the Holy Spirit is for me. I want *everything* You have for me, not just half."

That study continued through 1975. So did the viewing of Christian television. And our business continued to grow.

Nineteen seventy-five also marked the year that we moved into our Wolf Laurel chalet. It was like a mountain paradise with rustic exposed beams and a stone fireplace. After a year of planning and building and weekend retreats to oversee construction, moving in was a special treat.

We felt that we deserved a weekend and vacation hideaway, especially with the pressures of our weekday, workday ventures.

So when Christmas 1975 came, we made plans to spend it at the chalet. There would be plenty of parties, dancing, and eating. After all the school plays and festivities in Charlotte were finished, we piled into the Jeep Wagoneer with our collie and two siamese cats. We had packed all the ski clothes, and we could hardly contain our excitement. We knew that it would be a picture-perfect Christmas. Wolf Laurel is 5500 feet high, so we were hoping for snow during the vacation—lots of it.

Mr. Gosnell, a neighbor at Wolf Laurel, promised the children that he would help them cut down a

Christmas tree. We found out that when he said "tree," he really meant a *tree*! Our living room in the chalet was two stories high with massive poplar beams at the top—in all, the ceiling was eighteen feet high at the lowest point. Mr. Gosnell, Bill, and the kids came trudging in with this huge tree, and when they lifted it up and the top brushed the ceiling, the whole aura of Christmas really came alive. The smells of cooking and greenery, the sounds of banter and silver bells, the rustling of wrapping paper—who can adequately describe Christmas?

The entire Christmas season was one long party. We went to neighbors' homes, and they came for a big tree-trimming party at our chalet—fifty people in all were there.

Then, on Christmas Eve, after a last-minute shopping trip to nearby Asheville, we had just walked into our chalet when snowflakes began falling. Within an hour, there was a fresh, fluffy, white blanket of snow over everything we could see outside. The kids were so excited—they had never seen a Christmas like this before.

Bill's mother, Nell, had come down to spend Christmas with us. She didn't share our excitement about the snow—it reminded her too much of West Virginia. But we loved it; we didn't get much snow in Charlotte.

Mr. Gosnell came over with some fresh kindling wood, and as he got a fire blazing in the stone fireplace, he also asked my son, Les, to play the guitar. All of us gathered around the fire to sing

Christmas carols and some of Mr. Gosnell's favorites like "Just a Closer Walk."

If someone had written a script of an ideal Christmas vacation, ours would have followed that script almost down to the letter.

So why wasn't I happy? I had anticipated and visualized our first mountain Christmas in the chalet; instead, I was bored and depressed.

All the partying left me unexplainably cold. It was unlike me, but I tried to keep my happy mask intact.

When Bill, his mother, and the children were out riding all over the mountain in the snow, trying out our new four-wheel-drive jeep, I had a lot of time to think as I sat beside the crackling fireplace.

We didn't have a TV there, so I was totally alone with my thoughts. I couldn't help thinking about all the changes in my life. I wondered about all the lives I had touched. So many of my dreams had come true, but what did it all mean? What about my commitment to God?

Then, too, I had begun experiencing heart palpitations. I was having some of those old, familiar dark feelings again. Obviously, my low blood sugar was out of control once more.

Most of all, I began realizing the most sobering thought of all—I was nearing the top—not just all my dreams, but the *impossible dream*—and still I kept wondering if this was all there was. I just didn't know what that "something more" could be.

That Christmas ended with me wondering more than ever.

The day I came home from the hospital with Becky, I was so sick and already losing my hair. I thought it would be my last picture with the children.

Dear "Grandma" Moore who helped keep our family together in those dark days.

On stage, Mr. G. presented us with a special award as one of the top ten distributors.

V.G. Gochneaur and his wife, Pat, rejoiced with us as we walked the "Royal Road to Riches" for the fifth time as number one distributors! *(Photo by Mort Tucker.)*

Our precious children as they were growing up. I
had recovered from my illness and could finally
be the mom they needed.

Our family today, rejoicing in all that God has done for us. (l
to r) David, me, Bill, Becky, and Les. (*Photo by Natalie
Simpson.*)

Bill and I have really been blessed to work together as a team through the years. *(Photo by Natalie Simpson.)*

Our lovely "dream" home in Rutherfordton — a far cry from the "holler" shack of long ago! *(Photo by Natalie Simpson.)*

An opportunity to minister on the PTL Club. (l to r)
Les, Tammy Bakker, Jim Bakker (host), and me.

The Lord has given me such a desire to share from His Word.

Serving Jesus — the most impossible dream of all — fulfilled. *(Photo by Joe Long.)*

Chapter Seventeen

One Impossible Dream Down

Nineteen seventy-five was *the year* that climaxed our drive to the top. We had gone through a destiny-filled decade, ten years of both agony and ecstasy. In January, 1976, at the Fashion Two-Twenty International Convention in Las Vegas, Bill and I walked the "Royal Road to Riches" to be hailed as the *number one distributors in the entire world!* It was an indescribable thrill as we heard Mr. V. G. Gochneaur's favorite song, "The Impossible Dream,"—it had become a theme for us, too:

> To dream the impossible dream,
>   To fight the unbeatable foe,
> To bear with unbearable sorrow,
>   To run where the brave dare not go.
>
> To right the unrightable wrong,
>   To love, pure and chaste from afar,
> To try when your arms are too weary,
>   To reach the unreachable star!

This is my quest—to follow that star,
No matter how hopeless, no matter how far;
To fight for the right without question or
pause;
To be willing to march into hell for a heavenly
cause!

And I know if I'll only be true to this glorious
quest,
That my heart will lie peaceful and calm when
I'm laid to my rest,

And the world will be better for this;
That one man, scorned and covered with scars,
Still strove with his last ounce of courage,
To reach the unreachable star.

So much of our success was due, in a large part,
to our company's founder, Mr. V. G. Gochneaur.
He put new meaning into the words "help" and
"inspiration." He just couldn't do enough for people that he felt were willing to work. I had often
heard Mr. G. say, "One day I would like to go
down as a man who gave the most people the opportunity to rise above mediocrity."

His desire was for people to make it like he had.
He was a sharecropper's son with only an eighth
grade education, but by middle-age, he had become
a multi-millionaire. Yet, he had a compassion for
people. We were grateful—more at that coronation

moment than ever before—for Mr. G.'s part in helping us fulfill our impossible dream.

The super-high we were on in Las Vegas lasted all the way home. But even as we shared our elation with the children, our friends, and consultants, we realized that we would have to throw ourselves even more into the business. The top of the heap always belongs to the tenacious! The previous number one distributors would be striving to regain their niche; other fast-moving distributors would be climbing up the glass mountain. We were more determined than ever.

The beginning of 1976 started great; business was booming. We had every intention of repeating our triumph as the reigning number one distributors.

But there was trouble in paradise, too. For starters, we got a phone call from Wolf Laurel that our kind neighbor, Mr. Gosnell, had been killed in a fireworks accident. That made our impromptu Christmas hymn-singing even more bittersweet. I couldn't help thinking how empty my busy life seemed beside his deep, simple Christian walk.

I had made my own commitments to God, but they seemed so shallow and unvictorious. I wanted to do right and live like I should, but I just never seemed able to do it consistently.

But I kept struggling and hoping. I kept hearing on the Christian talk show that there *was* "something more." They continued talking about the "baptism of the Holy Spirit."

During the past year, since the evangelist's visit at the Coliseum, I had continued reading my Bible about this strange, "new" doctrine. I began underlining in red all of the places that mentioned the Holy Spirit. As I read and reread the Bible from Genesis to Revelation that year, I became aware that my Bible was becoming filled with red marks. I couldn't believe how many times the Holy Spirit was mentioned. He's on nearly every page of the New Testament. And I was shocked to see that Jesus always referred to the Holy Spirit as "He," not "it." Why had I heard so little about the Holy Spirit who was just as important as the other two parts of the Godhead (God the Father and God the Son)?

I continued searching the Scriptures—reading over and over again the passages that spoke about the Holy Spirit and this "baptism":

In Acts 2:1-21, the Holy Spirit came into the Upper Room like a mighty rushing wind as the disciples waited.

In Acts 8:4-17, Philip preached a revival and then Peter and John followed after to lay hands on the new converts so that they might receive the Holy Spirit.

In Acts 9, Saul (soon to be named Paul) was filled with the Holy Spirit after Ananias laid hands on him.

In Acts 10:34-36, Cornelius received the Holy

Spirit and began speaking in tongues just like the disciples did on the day of Pentecost.

In Acts 19:1-6, Paul laid hands on the Ephesian Christians, after which they were filled with the Holy Spirit and began to worship God in languages they did not know.

There were so many places outside of Acts, too; like 1 Corinthians 12, 13, and 14, and Luke 3:16 (when Jesus promised to do the very thing that later began happening on and after the day of Pentecost).

I read in Acts 2:16-18:

"...what you see this morning was predicted centuries ago by the prophet Joel—'In the last days,' God said, 'I will pour out my Holy Spirit upon all mankind, and your sons and daughters shall prophesy, and your young men shall see visions, and your old men dream dreams. Yes, the Holy Spirit shall come upon all my servants, men and women alike, and they shall prophesy'" (*The Living Bible*).

Obviously the Holy Spirit was for the "last days" too, and for *all* His servants—men and women alike.

Peter, in Acts 2:39, had promised the Holy Spirit to believers—"...for the promise is unto you, and to your children, and unto all them afar off, even as many as the Lord our God shall call!"

And I was astonished at the many places "speaking in tongues" and the baptism of the Holy Spirit were linked in Scripture.

I saw in Mark 16:17 that Jesus gave a special anointing as part of the Great Commission: "In my name they will cast out demons, they will speak in new tongues." Paul wrote in 1 Corinthians 14:5, "Now I wish that you all spoke in tongues," and in 1 Corinthians 14:18, "I thank God, I speak in tongues more than you all."

I studied Mark 16 where Jesus said that signs and wonders would follow them that believe. I saw no mention anywhere about a 2,000 year barrier on signs, wonders, tongues, or the baptism of the Holy Spirit.

The more I read the Bible, the more simple and plain it became. The gifts that the Holy Spirit gave, all of them, even a new, heavenly, prayer language, were for *all* who believed, not just a select few.

I found myself wanting this "baptism" more than any material thing. For years, beginning when I knelt at the altar at that little West Virginia church when I was a girl of fifteen, I had wanted all the blessings of God. But I had been sidetracked so long, hungry so long.

Through the TV program, and especially through studying Scriptures, I began to realize that by faith (Galatians 3:2), I could receive the person of the Holy Spirit and begin to experience a new, greater, and more joyful relationship with my Lord.

During my studies and times with God, I began to grasp some incredible truths. When I tried sharing some of them, I met with varied reactions. One woman said, "Wilda, why don't you just leave well enough alone? You're gonna keep on and get into trouble. A lot of those pentecostal-types have a counterfeit from Satan. You've already got Jesus. The Holy Spirit is with you and directing you. Now, just leave well enough alone!"

But I was too spiritually hungry to be stopped. I had gotten a taste of that wonderful joy from watching Christian television, and I had tasted even more from the Word. I wasn't about to stop now. I never was one to nibble at a little piece of the pie; I wanted all I could get!

I knew Jesus lived in my heart, but I wanted Him to be my best friend. I wanted Him—through the gift of the Holy Spirit—to give me joy and power like the parade of people had on TV.

I had tried to fool God and everyone else with my happy and satisfied masks for so many years, and I wasn't about to return to that. I wanted a true joy directly from the Source!

And I refused to be afraid. If some people did indeed have a counterfeit, then there must obviously be an original, and I knew that, according to Luke 11:11-13, God wouldn't hand out a false Holy Spirit to His children:

"You men who are fathers—if your boy asks for bread, do you give him a stone? If he asks for fish, do you give him a snake? If he asks for an egg, do you give him a scorpion? (Of course not!)

"And if even sinful persons like yourselves give

143

children what they need, don't you realize that your heavenly Father will do at least as much, and give the Holy Spirit to those who ask for Him?" (*The Living Bible*).

By the fall of 1977, and after another dry revival in our church, we finally decided to look around for a church where we could see the same joy we experienced watching the TV program.

We did find that church. We knew as soon as we entered the door that we had come to the right place. I saw hands being lifted during the worship service (I had seen that in Old Testament passages). We could actually *feel* the presence of the Lord there. I had read that God inhabits the praises of His people, and God was obviously pleased with the praises of that Sunday morning—He was there!

The next Thursday, I made a point to go to the midweek service at the same church. I didn't want to miss anything; plus, I was getting hungrier every day to receive this special baptism. I took Becky along, and sure enough—the pastor taught about the baptism of the Holy Spirit.

He laid it out so beautifully, explaining that I had to receive the Holy Spirit on the Lord's terms, not any man-made formulas. I had to totally abdicate the throne of my life to Him. He taught that God, for some reason, had chosen the tongue to be the most powerful instrument in the body (and thus, the hardest part to surrender). Apparently, for that reason, the gift of a heavenly language was a vital sign of this fresh indwelling.

At the end of the service, he wanted all who desired prayer for this gift to sit on the front pew. Becky and I were among twenty-five or so who went to the front. Obviously, I wasn't the only one wanting to know more about this special walk with God.

The pastor walked across the front laying hands on each head, praying for us, encouraging us to relax and praise God. One by one, as we surrendered even our tongues to the Lord God, we each received that unspeakable gift.

"...Jesus shouted to the crowds, 'If anyone is thirsty, let him come to me and drink. For the Scriptures declare that rivers of living water shall flow from the inmost being of anyone who believes in me.' (He was speaking of the Holy Spirit, who would be given to everyone believing in Him...)" (John 7:37-39, *The Living Bible*).

I heard my own voice joining in the praise, then I heard myself speaking a language I had never learned. It was so unfamiliar, yet I felt overwhelmed with a beautiful love for everyone. Everyone!

I saw my little Becky beside me lifting her hands, worshipping and praising God in a heavenly language also. It reminded me of what I had read in Acts 2:4: "And everyone present was filled with the Holy Spirit and began speaking in languages they didn't know, for the Holy Spirit gave them this ability."

We were having our own day of Pentecost. It was worship in the purest form. I don't know how long we were there, but for the first time in my life, I had a real *joy* bubbling out of my soul. It was a joy unspeakable and full of glory.

I had found something that I had searched for all of my life. I hadn't found joy in all my other dreams. I had only partially found peace in my decisions made for Christ at other times in my life, and each time I had been discouraged when I fell so short of what I felt God wanted me to be. I always had to bolster my faith up by myself.

But that night, when I received the baptism of the Holy Spirit, I knew deep down in my soul that I had tapped into the Source. It wasn't flowing out of me—manufactured by me; instead, it was flowing *through* me. It wasn't me, but Him. What a difference.

I found that I couldn't get enough of the Bible. I practically devoured it each day during the coming months. For the next two years, I had an insatiable thirst for the Word of God. I wanted to know about God, everything about Him. I had missed so much.

And another thing startled me—I suddenly couldn't keep myself from telling others about Christ. This certainly wasn't the old Wilda Sue—I had always been shy and self-conscious about such things.

What a difference that night made when I received the Holy Spirit's baptism.

I had no idea what a difference that "Someone Else" would make.

Chapter Eighteen

The Fire Spreads

Becky and I rejoiced all the way home from that service. Bill and the boys were sitting in the den watching a "shoot-em-up" on the tube. Our grand announcement—"We've both been baptized in the Holy Spirit!"—got no response.

I hoped that they just hadn't heard. I raised my voice the din of the television. "Bill, we went forward tonight for prayer, and the pastor prayed for Jesus to baptize us in the Holy Spirit. We've both received our prayer language!"

Bill looked up for a moment—"You did? That's good."

I was mystified at his lack of emotion, but it was a quick lesson in personal Christianity that I would face again and again: Until a person experiences such a step himself, he can't really relate to what another person is saying.

I also quickly realized that God had given me a special love. Before, I would have defended myself in such a situation, but tonight I just felt love. During the coming days, I found that I loved Bill more than I had ever loved him before. My love grew deeper for my children; I grew interested in *their* lives and what *they* wanted to talk about, not just my own goals. No longer was it a mere ritual to make myself listen to what was important to them—their own dreams, their hobbies, incidents at school. Things like that became important to me, too.

In reading the Bible and praying with a new joy, I noticed that I was becoming sensitive to the Holy Spirit's leading. I could tell when He was quickening me as I prayed in the Spirit, and it became a thrilling faith-walk to see that He was interested in sharing His truths with me.

But, I found that this new walk with Christ was filled with a lot of things that I had not been totally prepared for. One of the laws of physics is this: "For every action, there is an equal and opposite reaction." The same, I found, is true in the spiritual arena. I quickly became aware that there was not only a Holy Spirit, but that there was an unholy spirit as well.

I hadn't thought about Satan much, but he was right in the Bible:

"For we wrestle not against flesh and blood, but against principalities, against powers, against the rulers of the darkness of this world, against spiritual wickedness in high places" (Ephesians 6:12).

"The thief (Satan) cometh not, but for to steal,

and to kill, and to destroy: I (Jesus) am come that they might have life, and that they might have it more abundantly" (John 10:10).

I had gone one step deeper with God. Satan hated me even more than when I was just a nominal Christian. Before, when I tried doing everything in my own power, I was no threat to him, but when I became overflowing with the Holy Spirit, I was a problem. I found that he would stop at nothing to try to get me to back up into the spiritual uselessness I had known for so long.

The first attack came personally—"Are you sure you aren't just making up that 'heavenly' language? You're just puppeting something you've heard somewhere!"

When that didn't work, then the attacks came on my family. All three of our children have always been very musically inclined. Les learned to play the guitar very early, and David took lessons, too. Becky took piano lessons. They all had unusual talent as singers as well.

Les was seventeen and had become involved as the lead singer and lead guitarist with a rock band he had helped form. All of the boys in the group were extremely talented and were putting together a terrific, tight sound.

We were really proud of Les, at first. It seemed a wholesome and creative activity. But now, he lived and breathed music—his bedroom was constantly throbbing with *Kiss* and *Queen*. I began to realize that, as a Christian, the world of rock music wasn't for him, especially the dives and sleazy clubs where his group would probably have to play.

I no longer felt a peace about Les playing in that group. It wasn't just a personal preference; I increasingly felt the quickening of the Holy Spirit in this.

I was asked to attend a meeting at our house with his group not long after I was baptized in the Holy Spirit. The group had an agent who was going to "make 'em famous," but of course they had to have an adult sign the booking contract. Well, right in front of the whole group, I refused to sign. At that moment, I knew Les was at a crucial point in his life—one that he might never come to again.

Naturally, Les was furious with me, partly for refusing to sign but mostly for embarrassing him in front of his friends. He refused to even talk to me, but I was determined more than ever that Satan wouldn't have the opportunity to use Les' God-given talents. Les didn't know it, but I began interceding for him before the Lord, binding the enemy from his life and releasing God's love and the Holy Spirit upon him.

From all appearances, the opposite was true. Les inherited his determination from me, so we were at a stalemate. My dream to have him perform God's music seemed more impossible than ever.

Our family was planning to go to my younger sister Joyce's home in Ohio for Thanksgiving that year. Just a few days before we left, Les came up to me and began talking, matter of factly, just as though we had never had the face-off and freeze. It seemed that he had been reading a book, *The Cross and the Switchblade*, by David Wilkerson. For whatever reason, the book had been used to touch his heart. He realized that he needed the power of the Holy Spirit to serve God.

We talked seriously about the Holy Spirit—the mere fact that we were talking was special to both of us.

Then we left for Warren, Ohio, to spend the Thanksgiving holidays with about twenty-five family members at Joyce's house. Even in the five-bedroom house, there seemed to be wall-to-wall people, especially as it came time for the festive dinner.

That day, to our surprise, we found out that Joyce had received the baptism of the Holy Spirit two years before. We had plenty to talk about! Before Thanksgiving Day was over, we had turned her master bedroom into a literal "upper room" as one of the guests and Les received the baptism of the Holy Spirit and began praising God in a language they had never learned.

That was a clear signal that God was overshadowing our lives, carefully guiding every contact, even on a Thanksgiving vacation.

After we left Joyce's, we went by Columbus, Ohio, to visit Claire, the woman who had sent me the copy of *Good News For Modern Man* when I was locked in that dark pit. Claire was one of my early recruits who was not only a good friend, but one who had gone on to be one of the top managers within the company. God was doing something great in her life as well.

After dinner, Bill held a cigarette up and mentioned, "You know, I'd give anything if I could quit these things."

Claire, our friend, said, "Do you really mean that, Bill?"

When he nodded, she stood up and laid her hands on his head, praying for deliverance from his two and one-half pack-a-day tobacco habit. Bill had tried to quit many times, but didn't have the will-power. I had only recently been delivered myself from the same habit.

Well, this time for Bill was obviously different. Not only was that the last cigarette Bill ever touched, but in the days to come, he never experienced any of the normal withdrawal symptoms or cravings!

Then Claire's husband, Ray, showed us his sound system and his collection of Gospel soundtracks (musical background tapes). Ray didn't know it, but his tapes were an answer to prayer. Increasingly, I had felt God's calling for me and my family to use our musical talents for the Lord, but taking along cumbersome guitar amplifiers and equipment didn't seem like the answer. Besides, it had been years since I had played the guitar. Ray's thorough explanation of these relatively new orchestration tapes formed the foundation of a direction I felt the Lord would lead me into in the near future. I was amazed—even in such a simple thing as tapes—that I could see God's hand, that He had everything planned and in control.

When we left Claire and Ray's home, it began peppering down snow. By evening, cars were pulling off the road because of the deep snow and icy spots, so we decided to stop for the night. Unfortunately, everyone else had the same idea; every motel that we came to had no vacancies. Finally, I said: "Well, we have nothing to lose, so let's pray about finding a room." That certainly was not the old Wilda talking! We asked God for a room, and the very next exit we got off had a motel with one room left—only one! We knew it was more than just a coincidence.

The next day, we lost our gas cap after stopping at a service station. We went back and looked all over for it, but to no avail. Bill and the boys were getting chilled as the cold wind whipped around them. Again, with nothing to lose, we prayed and asked God to show us His wisdom even in such a small thing as a gas cap. Almost immediately, Bill found some money on the ground to pay for a brand new cap. As I watched him bend over to pick up those bills, I was amazed at God's concern over every area of our lives.

It certainly wasn't the money that blessed me.

We could have easily bought a cap without going back to look for the lost one. But God let us see that He was concerned about every single thing in our lives, that His hand was on everything. And He was teaching us to trust Him in everything.

To many Christians, things like a motel room, a lost gas cap, and soundtracks are so small they certainly shouldn't be included in a story, but to us, each time it was like a direct revelation from God. We hadn't known that He was truly concerned about such day-to-day things. It was a breath of fresh life.

We already knew that God could handle big things. One evening, I went to visit my family—my parents and my sister Carol's family had both moved to western North Carolina by then. In my haste, as I left Carol's house, I drank a glass of tea with sugar in it—a definite "no-no" for anyone with hypoglycemia. On the way back to Charlotte, I became very weak and had a bad spell of heart palpitations. Somehow I kept driving, and as I did, I heard a voice very plainly say, "You don't have to have hypoglycemia!" That's all I heard, but I knew it was God's voice. When I got home, Bill and David were watching our favorite Christian talk show. I was still weak, but I decided to watch for awhile, too.

There was a woman being interviewed—Vicki Jamison. I had heard of her before, but had never seen her ministering or on television. She was talking about God's healing power. When she started praying, I could feel God's presence in our den. I looked at Bill; his head was bowed.

Vicki finished praying, then began calling out specific problems that were being healed in the audience: "Someone's back problem is being healed in the name of Jesus...and sir, God is touching your eyes..."

Without thinking, I reached out my hand and said, "hypoglycemia," and at that *exact* moment she said, "Someone in the television audience is being healed of hypoglycemia right now!"

Suddenly God's power touched me. I felt warm electricity flow over my entire body. I had been touched by His healing power just as certainly as the woman who touched the hem of Jesus' garment and was made whole.

Needless to say, my family was thrilled! We had previously adjusted our lives around my hypoglycemia. The next day, just to see if I was truly healed (although I don't suggest that anyone make this a habit!), I drank a coke and ate a doughnut during a break in my activities. Nothing happened! I was amazed at what I could eat and drink from that point on, although God has greatly tempered my eating habits into healthy ones since then!

Between the television program and the Thanksgiving trip, God was showing a special interest in everything that we did. He also had a few surprises.

One involved money. Since I was taking a leave of absence from the studio to spend the summer vacation with my children, I had saved exactly a thousand dollars so that we would have plenty of money for the things we would be doing over the summer. But, as I counted the money, I heard God plainly say, "That's not yours." I shot back, "Yes, it is! I saved it for our special time together, and we are going to have lots of fun with it."

Well, that same night, we were watching the Christian television program. They were having a fund-raising telethon to pay for the use of a satellite to take the Gospel to the world.

I thought, "How wonderful that we even have that kind of technology. It's exciting to be able to reach so many people. I sure hope a lot of people send in money so that people all over the world can be blessed like we are in America."

Then I heard God speak to me—"Wilda, *you* give the thousand dollars."

"Me, give the thousand?" I replied. "Oh, no I'm not! It's mine and the kids—it's our spending money. I'm not about to give it away." And I dismissed it from my mind.

The next day was Saturday. The telethon on TV lasted for several hours, so I sat down to watch. From my seat in the den, I could see Bill and the children outside on the patio. They were laughing and having a great time playing some game.

Suddenly, I felt God's presence in the den with

me. I remembered myself as a little girl in the West Virginia church, and I could vividly recall the tremendous sacrifice that I made one Sunday when I put one shiny dime into the collection plate—a wooden plate with a burgandy pad inside. As I looked into the plate, I had to make a momentous decision since I probably wouldn't have a dime again for some time, but still I dropped it on the pad.

Then, those scenes dissolved like an antique mirage when God said to me, "Wilda, *then* you gave ten pennies; *now* you give ten one hundreds."

I knew God meant business. He wanted my obedience more than my words. When I surrendered that special thousand dollars, I felt a warmth of love flow through me.

The next day after church, I told Bill about the telethon gift I wanted to make. I had no idea what his reaction would be.

"Wilda, are you *sure* God told you to give that much?" he asked.

"Yes, I'm very sure."

"Well, if you're sure, give me the money you've saved, and I'll put it in the bank so you can send them a check."

I didn't give that money expecting to receive anything in return, but I soon learned that God is always faithful to His Word. He means it when He says, "Give and it shall be given to you..."

The very next Friday, we went on a trip we had been planning to Hilton Head Island, South

Carolina. Bill wanted to buy a villa there for an investment. We were learning how to do things God's way: we started the venture with prayer. When we found the villa we wanted, we immediately prayed that God's will would be done. Bill's offer, which we believed was fair, was less than the asking price, but the owner accepted the offer. To top it off, we sold the villa in a year and a half for $24,000 more than we had paid for it! God had shown us how to make a sound investment.

He was dramatically showing us, step by step, that He was in control. Nothing was too hard for Him—not property purchases, not personal problems. And nothing was too small for His attention.

In the coming months, I saw Becky healed of chronic nightmares. I saw Bill healed of painful headaches (though he still had many reservations about the baptism of the Holy Spirit).

We saw God continue to bless our business as never before. Each year we were named the number one distributors in the world of Fashion Two-Twenty.

There were problems, of course. Bill and I had arguments that we never had before. We had to make decisions that we never had to make before, but we had a guidance from the Holy Spirit that we never had before.

God's Word was real. The baptism of the Holy Spirit was *working*. God did indeed hear and answer prayers just like He did two thousand years ago.

We were growing and prospering in His Spirit. Could it possibly get any better?

Chapter Nineteen

Acres of Dreams

Bill and I had always dreamed of owning a farm someday, a place where we could enjoy nature and let our children learn about life outside the city.

When Bill heard about forty-two acres of country property for sale in Rutherford County, North Carolina, we decided to see if it was what we had dreamed of owning. Was it ever! Once called the Hampton Plantation, the land was nestled in the Carolina foothills with purple mountains rising in the background. Lush foliage, red maple trees, white oak trees, one huge hickory-nut tree, and all the surrounding hillsides were dotted with spectacular greenery.

When I was just a small girl, I had mentioned to my daddy that I would someday like to live in a big, white, Southern colonial home on a farm with cows all around on green hills.

Well, as we stood on this piece of property, I could instantly visualize that exact childhood dream. We made the owners an offer which they accepted, and we began a life of transition.

The move meant endless hours of overseeing the construction of our house, barn, and fences. We moved our business headquarters to Shelby (halfway between Charlotte and Rutherfordton), more centrally located in our Carolina-Tennessee franchise area. We had to move our children from the prestigious Carmel Academy in Charlotte to public schools in Rutherford County (and since Les' senior year was coming up, it made the change even harder).

As soon as we decided to build on the property, we immediately listed our Charlotte home, but it went for months without selling. We were getting a little unnerved. "Had we made a mistake? Had we missed God's leading?" It had seemed so right for us to make the move. Finally, after months of going without a sale, we decided to take the realty sign down; maybe the time wasn't quite right yet.

Then, shortly after we took the sign down, I heard God speak as I was making our bed one morning—"Your house is going to be sold!"

I was puzzled, of course. "How can that be? We've even taken our house off the market."

But sure enough, it happened. Big homes were scarce at the time in Charlotte, and that same week *two* out-of-town families came to town looking for a home like ours. Since our home had previously been on sale, the real estate people called to see if we would consider selling.

Would we? The house sold that same week! Immediately, we contacted a contractor to begin our dream home in Rutherford County.

However, the new owners of the Charlotte house wanted possession long before our new home would be finished. We had no choice except to store our furniture in Charlotte and temporarily move up to our Wolf Laurel chalet.

What a summer! Bill was trying to keep the business going and all our managers and studios supplied. We were attempting to live normally, while intermittently scattered between our construction site in Rutherford County, our chalet in Wolf Laurel, our old headquarters in Charlotte, and our new headquarters in Shelby. How we stayed relatively sane, I'll never know! In each place, though, God opened more and more doors to tell people about what Jesus had done for us.

Then, when school began, we found a temporary place to stay near our new house (still under construction) in Rutherford County—a little farmhouse that hadn't been lived in for eight years. That was the beginning of something extremely beautiful in my life. It was there in that old farmhouse that I realized that I didn't have to have materialistic things, comforts, and modern conveniences to be happy. In fact, it was the happiest three months of my life. We just set up housekeeping with what was already inside the dusty farmhouse—everything we owned was either in storage in Charlotte or in our

Wolf Laurel chalet.

There was a little refrigerator, one of the first invented, with no door on the freezer compartment. The old cooking stove had the oven burnt out and stove-top burners that would only burn on high. The old beds were much too short for my six feet, two inch tall Bill. The dishes and cooking utensils looked just like the ones we had used when I was a child. The fuses kept blowing, so we spent a large part of the evenings trying to replace the fuses while fumbling in the dark. The old well kept breaking down. Then, when late fall came, we had no heat except one old wood stove—we almost froze.

For the old Wilda of just a short time before, ugly memories of the "holler" shack would have driven me into hysterics and/or depression, but I found myself lifted above the circumstances. I was more amazed than anyone to see that God had healed the deep scars that had been forged from those tormented childhood years. I was rejoicing in circumstances that would have made me miserable before. I was learning—with God's help—to be with and to be without. I realized that my time in this old farmhouse, without luxuries, was going to be relatively short, but I was still thrilled that the throbbing ache in my heart had been healed.

In November, after five and a half months of being uprooted, we put the finishing touches on our "dream" home and moved our furniture into the waiting rooms. We had gone to a lot of extra trouble

to make it a dream fulfilled—two specially con-
structed two-story spiral staircases, custom-made
redwood columns painted white for the front of the
house, imported tile, custom cabinets, fifteen rooms,
a salt-cured pine deck leading to our kidney-shaped
swimming pool, and a view from my kitchen window that would have stunned Michelangelo. All of
the furniture that we bought for our Charlotte home
had been purchased with our dream home in mind,
and our dream had finally come true.

This was the big Southern colonial home that I
had pictured as a child—the same one that I told my
daddy I would live in someday.

We celebrated Thanksgiving exactly one week
after we moved in, and then we had to hustle to get
ready for the Christmas holidays—shopping, decorating, planning, dreaming. My parents and two of
my sisters and their families had moved to North
Carolina and lived less than an hour and half away,
so they were all planning to have dinner with us on
Christmas Day and exchange gifts then. We were so
happy, not just to be getting ready for Christmas,
but to be settled into one place, not running so
much.

As Christmas approached, the house was a
splendid tribute to our family's decorating efforts—
a blue-spruce tree gaily decorated in the family
room, garlands of red-velvet bows draped down the
winding stairways.

On Christmas Eve morning, Bill was planning

to go to Charlotte to get David, who had been visiting with a friend, and Les was going to Asheville to finish his last-minute shopping. Everybody was in a festive mood. Bill and Becky were playing in the den while I continued my dinner preparations for the next day.

I heard Bill say, "Becky, Daddy wants to rest awhile." He saw me standing at the door—"Wilda, I think I have indigestion or something. I'm going to lie down and rest for a few minutes, okay?"

I went back to my baking, thinking about the different things I needed to do before our company arrived.

Becky went upstairs to make her bed, and I heard Bill say that he would help her. Shortly, Becky came running back down the stairs.

"Mommy! Mommy! Come quick! Daddy said his heart's hurting!"

I ran up the steps swiftly, trying to ignore the fearful thoughts rushing through my mind.

Bill had staggered into Les' room and was lying across the bed. The pain was intolerable—I could see that etched on his face. I almost panicked, but somehow kept the presence of mind to pray for him first, then phoned our neighbor.

Ray and his wife, Joann, came over immediately, and Ray raced Bill to the nearest emergency room. By the time they reached the hospital, Bill was barely breathing.

I had to wait behind until Suzette, Ray's

daughter, could come to watch Becky. By the time Joann and I did arrive at the hospital, the doctor was waiting with serious news. Bill had experienced a severe heart attack. Yet, even though a fourth of his heart was gone, he was still managing to stay alive.

When I could finally go into his room, I wasn't prepared for what I saw. Just a short time before, my husband had been playing with Becky. Now, he had an ominous oxygen tube in his nose; his face was swollen and puffy. I took his hand, and he turned toward me with big, hot tears trickling down his face. He said, "Wilda, I prayed to God, that He wouldn't let me die. I asked Him to let me live and raise my children."

I tried to sound courageous: "Honey, you're not going to die; you're going to live. God's not through with us yet."

That quick exchange of words kept me going during a strangely quiet Christmas. We exchanged presents; the kids were so brave; our company came, and we ate (or at least picked at) the prepared foods and goodies—but it was all so meaningless without Bill. The kids and I were just moping around with long faces. There was always that unspoken question—"Would he come home?"

I had to make myself stop and see how we were acting. I gathered the kids around and told them that we had to start acting more thankful. "After all," I reminded them, "Daddy is alive—not dead like many men who have heart attacks in their early forties. We have to have faith that Daddy will come home safely to us."

I spent as much time as possible (five minutes every hour) on Christmas Eve and Christmas Day with Bill; he was in so much pain and still in very, very, serious condition.

In answer to prayer, the hospital let the children in to see Bill on Christmas Day. It was a special blessing for them, and it really encouraged their daddy.

The day after Christmas, I kept beating a path between our home and the hospital. That evening, when I went in for my allotted five minutes, it was a different Bill that I saw. He had a radiant face, his cheeks were rosy, his eyes were sparkling— "Wilda," he exclaimed, "God healed me while you were gone!"

I tried to keep my composure as he outlined the visit from a pastor, Sam Whaley, who had come at our neighbor Ray's request.

The pastor had quoted Isaiah 53:5, "with his stripes we are healed," and a similar verse in 1 Peter 2:24. Then he laid his hands on Bill's chest and prayed. Bill related, "I felt something in my chest, like fingers inside moving around as he prayed. By the time he said, 'Amen!' the pain was completely gone!"

It was almost too good to believe, but I knew that God could do it—we had gone through too much to doubt Him. When I had to leave Bill's room, I was praising God for the obvious healing, thrilled to know my precious husband was going to live. God was so wonderfully good!

On the way out, the charge nurse stopped me. "Mrs. Marple, some preacher came in and prayed for your husband. And now Mr. Marple thinks he is healed!"

When I told her how happy I was that he was so much better, she gave me an icy look of disgust. "Mrs. Marple," she intoned, "whether you know it or not, your husband has just had a severe heart attack and a fourth of his heart is completely dead. I've seen men die with much better chances than he has. I'm warning you to talk some sense into him!"

The next morning they moved Bill out of the intensive care unit and into a private room. The following day he unhooked his monitor (the nurses watching the monitoring equipment down the hall panicked, thinking his heart had stopped!), went down to the bathroom, and took a shower. He had been told not to even lift his arms to shave, much less get up and walk around!

The orderlies and nurses never did give up trying to get him to be more cautious. They were all amazed that he could even walk without huffing and puffing.

When the doctors ran a series of tests, they were astounded to discover that there was absolutely nothing wrong with his heart, no damage whatsoever! (Any doctor's checkups in the years since then have revealed the same miraculous results!)

In the hospital, Bill told everyone about the healing hand of God.

I took his Bible in, and every time I would go in, he would be so excited about something new he had found. "Wilda, did you know that the Bible says that all things work together for good to them that love God and are called according to His purpose?" (Romans 8:28). I had quoted Scriptures to him many times, but it had never been such a personally revealed thing to him before.

There were still problems, of course, and we have never reached perfection (does anyone?), but one fact was crystal clear—God had intervened dramatically in our lives, once again.

Our life had been a chain of miracles and struggles. Both Bill and I had reached the end—we had stared death in the face, and both of us had been given another opportunity to live. We would never be the same again as a result.

When Bill was released from the hospital on January 5, 1979, we found that even though we had missed the Fashion Two-Twenty International Convention for the first time, we had been recognized for the fourth year in a row as the number one distributors in the company.

We went back to our dream home more grateful and thankful than ever. Even Bill was extremely aware that God was overshadowing our walk—for some special purpose.

Chapter Twenty

The Team

Bill and I had always made such a great team. When we got married, he wanted it to work because of his tragic first marriage, and I responded accordingly because my childhood memories reminded me of how a marriage could be either heaven or hell. We both wanted it to be something special, and it was.

There were hard times, of course, especially when Bill was laid off by Union Carbide. But we grew closer through the good *and* bad.

When we got into the business together, we found that our common goal brought us even closer as friends, lovers, parents, and partners.

I was always one-hundred percent gung ho for anything I did, while Bill ran at a more even "keel." The balance worked well. Our success proved that.

But when I was baptized in the Holy Spirit, quite frankly, it caused some trouble for our team in the beginning. Unfortunately, we went through a sequence of hurts, trials, and disappointments for both of us.

171

Bill had always seen me go full-force for anything I was interested in: my business (I had to go to the top no matter what stood in my way), reading (once I got on such a "kick" of reading that I nearly drove Bill crazy with my non-stop habit), and health foods. There was no in-between for me. It was all or nothing.

So, when I got involved in the move of the Holy Spirit, Bill thought he saw my usual "gung ho" pattern surface. He just figured that I was on another "kick," and that I would come down from it after awhile. This truly hurt me because I so wanted us to continue being a team—especially in the Holy Spirit. I wanted us to be on the same spiritual plane. Even with his first responses, I figured that it would only be a matter of time before he would come into the baptism of the Holy Spirit. How wrong I was.

Bill heard me say that I was healed when Vicki Jamison called out "hypoglycemia" during the telecast, but he just thought that I was being emotional. Even when I had no more spells with heart palpitations and queasiness, and when I could eat sweets again (though I have since learned better), he was still wondering when I would get involved in another "kick."

When he developed a headache while we were going to Hilton Head, and when the tormenting pain left him after I laid hands on his head and prayed, he began to realize that there was something to it—it was more than just a "kick"—but he was still skeptical.

When he was healed of his near-fatal heart attack, he really saw that healing was for him, for today. He saw that there really was something to the work of the Holy Spirit. During his hospital stay, he got quite involved with a personal study of the Bible. I was so excited—this had to be the turning point. I figured that it would now be time for Bill's baptism. We could be a real team again.

Sure enough, shortly after that, at a Full-Gospel convention in Asheville, Bill was slain in the Spirit and received his prayer language. I rejoiced with him. It was even better than I had hoped. That made me doubly unprepared for what unfolded next.

I'd like Bill to explain it now because he says it best:

"I did receive the baptism of the Holy Spirit, but Satan hit me quickly with the thought that I had made it all up—I had fallen down in the Spirit because everyone else had; I had puppeted something I heard.

"He really began working on me. It hurt my relationship with the Lord. It caused a lot of problems with Wilda. We had never fought much before, but we sure started after that.

"One of the worst times was at a Full-Gospel meeting in New Orleans. Although I had never been able to get involved with the charismatic services before—raising my hands, and worshipping outloud—I did some the first few nights.

"Then, the last night of the convention, it suddenly hit me how absurd all of it seemed. I looked around at fifteen thousand people praising God.

"'They're all nuts,' I said to myself. 'Wilda, our friends, everyone—I'm the only sane one in the whole bunch.'

"And at that moment, while surrounded by all those worshipping people, I decided that when we got back home, I would pack my bags and quickly get away from Wilda and all that charismatic stuff.

"I didn't, of course, but I didn't change much in my thoughts. Looking back, I realize that I let Satan steal my joy and freedom.

"I also realize why I reacted this way. I was always very conservative and self-conscious, maybe even timid. I always had a rough time letting loose with anything.

"Wilda was just the opposite. It was always so easy for her to let go. Especially when she got into the baptism of the Holy Spirit. It seemed so natural and perfect for her to be free.

"I began to get more and more resentful. She had something I didn't.

"During these months, I went through a real depression. I didn't even want to be around people.

"It was so hard to take—we had had so few marital problems through the years, then, because of the baptism in the Holy Spirit—suddenly things seemed to be in a turmoil.

"I didn't realize that what we were experiencing wasn't all that uncommon for couples newly introduced to the Holy Spirit. Often it is more difficult for the second one in a marriage to come into the baptism. Plus, the people involved are coming into a new dimension of the Spirit—one that Satan violently hates. He bids the highest stakes—he hates a couple that are able to move together in the Holy Spirit."

I had a real problem with Bill not being able to move ahead in the Spirit. I had always admired his masculinity, individualism, and stubbornness before. But now it seemed so frustrating, especially since I felt that those very attributes were hurting his relationship with the Lord.

It really came to a head on our twenty-first wedding anniversary. Ray and Joann Norville, our neighbors, asked us to go to Charlotte for PTL's combination *Labor Day Celebration* and *Heritage USA Dedication*. I wanted to go because our son, Les, was in a Christian music group by then, and they would be ministering there. But Bill refused to go. I'd like him to finish his story:

"I realized soon afterward that I was a victim of my own stubbornness. When it began sinking in that I had stood in the way of a special day in the Lord, I realized more than ever that I needed to let a part of me die.

"Wilda and I had been discussing our minister's sermons—dying to self. There were so many Scriptures that talked about that idea, especially in Romans.

"We prayed together, quoting Matthew 18:19, agreeing together that God was going to do a special work in me. I surrendered all of my self, so that Christ could live in me."

That was the beginning of a real turnaround for Bill, but there were still times of spiritual heaviness. Then, one winter night, as I was getting dinner ready, the Lord told me to fast for twenty-one days for Bill, that He was going to do a work in Bill's spiritual heart.

So, I began my Daniel Fast based on Daniel 10:2, eating greens and lentils, no sweets or meats.

After the first day of the fast, we went to bed, but early in the morning—two or three o'clock— Bill woke me up. He was looking out the window, "Someone must've rang the door bell."

There was no one at the door, so I didn't think too much about what happened. But while reading and meditating on the book of Daniel a few days later, my heart leaped as I read chapter ten, verse twelve: "Then he said, 'Don't be frightened, Daniel, for your request has been heard in heaven and was answered the very first day you began to fast before the Lord and pray for understanding; that very day I was sent here to meet you'" (*The Living Bible*).

To me it was a special sign that God had heard my request even during the first day of my fast. Bill had thought he heard something like music during the early morning hours, but I felt that God was showing me that He was already at work on Bill's spiritual heart.

And so I continued with the fast. We left to go to our home office advisory board meeting in Aurora, Ohio. The dinners were incredible feasts of thick, aromatic filet mignon and simmering prime rib, but I knew that it was important for me to continue my Daniel Fast; and at each meal there were plenty of greens to eat.

Slowly but surely, Bill began to change. Other people started noticing it, too—his growing concern for souls, a new ability to talk more openly about the Lord.

It wasn't necessarily my faith; God just wanted to show us both that He was in control. He wanted my obedience, and He wanted Bill to be aware that He was getting ready to move us into something very special.

More than that—we had become a team again.

Chapter Twenty-One

The Dreams Still Grow

Since 1976, when I decided to take more and more time off from Fashion Two-Twenty, I have experienced the most exciting times of my life. The time off, even with the move to Rutherfordton, gave me an opportunity to listen. I had never done a lot of that before, and to hear God, one often has to just be silent before Him.

So, I was very surprised when in January, 1980, while Bill and I were attending a New Orleans seminar, I felt a stir of excitement for the cosmetic business world for the first time in five years.

For half a decade, God had temporarily taken away my self-destructive desire to "make it" in the business. For one thing, we were at the top, and the people in our organization were continuing to grow and expand, so our own franchises were doing well without me having to push so hard. Bill kept it together well.

The most important reason why the desire left,

however, was so I would have time to "get my act together" with the Lord. For so long I had my priorities far out of balance. I had suffered the consequences and had paid a tremendous personal price for my share of success in the business world.

For over ten years, from 1965 to 1976, I had quite literally burned my candle at both ends, and, as a result, I had burned myself out—physically, mentally, and spiritually.

Everyone has a god. Some have religious gods, while others have more materialistic ones. For more than a decade, I lived, breathed, ate, slept, and thought about being number one—and staying number one. My children, husband, and Lord were somewhere down the list.

As a result of that obsessive drive, God took me away from my other god for five full years, and began a remolding process in me. It began with such simple things—way back with that first reading of *Good News for Modern Man* as I struggled to get out of the deep, dark pit. It continued as I watched Christian television and became aware of another world—a world where Jesus could be as close as the mention of His name.

This new walk continued through my own personal journey with the Holy Spirit, as I searched the Scriptures, and when I finally received that precious baptism myself.

The healings, the answers to prayer, small and large, the ways He brought my family along the same trail—all were bits and pieces of my education.

The interim period after we moved from Charlotte and were "forced" (because our dream home was still under construction) to live in our Wolf Laurel chalet was especially precious. It was such a switch to be there—so quiet, so peaceful, no shopping malls around to go to at night. When we moved there, the Lord told me, "I have you here to get your attention."

The kids stayed busy playing with their new-found friends, and Bill spent four days of the week back in Charlotte with the business, so I let my mind and spirit be saturated with the Word. For the first time, the Lord began to reveal some deep truths from the Bible. It seemed that the more I read and studied, the more the words came alive—almost dancing on the page.

Then, when we moved to the old farmhouse in Rutherford County, I realized that God had not only broken me into little pieces, but He had put me back together again. He had healed so many open "sores" that had hurt me all my life. I found that no longer did material things mean so much to me. The old farmhouse was a lot like I had been raised in (Becky loved it; she said it reminded her of the *Little House on the Prairie*). And it was a real signal that God had done a deep work in me.

During that time, He gave me a Scripture that has become my special prayer of thanks and praise. "O Lord, You alone are my hope; I've trusted You from childhood. Yes, You have been with me from birth and have helped me constantly—no wonder I am always praising You! My success—at which so many stand amazed—is because You are my mighty protector. All day long I'll praise and honor You, Oh God, for all that You have done for me" (Psalm 71:5-8, *The Living Bible*).

I could live with plenty, and I could live with very little—it no longer hurt. I was at peace either way.

So why, then, in 1980, would God be giving me a newfound enthusiasm for the cosmetic world? It was puzzling.

Slowly, I began to understand what the Lord was saying. He felt that I was finally back in balance and had my priorities right—God first, my husband second, then my children, my church, and finally, my business. "Seek ye first the Kingdom of God and his righteousness; and all these things shall be added unto you" (Matthew 6:33).

With that balance intact, God revealed that He would prosper our business even more than before. Bill and I began to realize that even though we have been the number one distributors in one of the most competitive businesses in the world, still we have only scratched the surface. With God at the throne of our business, who knows what can be done?

Soon after Bill and I talked about that, God opened up some unexpected doors. Fashion Two-Twenty had changed owners after all of those years, and Bill and I began to wonder if the Lord had something new for us.

Sure enough, acquaintances of ours who had founded their own cosmetic business a few years before were very much interested in us. They were delighted when we agreed to join their staff at *Lady Finelle*. I am working as a manager, with a company car, and Bill and I are working together as field persons.

Not only are our new positions challenging and exciting to us, but an area of reaching out to businesswomen with the good news of the Kingdom has opened up in an overwhelming way.

God has shown Bill and me that He needs people in business to be practical examples of His Word—"Beloved, I wish above all things that thou mayest prosper and be in health, even as thy soul prospereth" (3 John 2). God is not the God of poverty.

Also, He has shown us that He has been able to use me as an example that a successful businesswoman can also have her personal, marital, and spiritual life in order. I am living proof that any woman can rise above her circumstances and be successful. And my story is also an example of what happens when God is left out of that success!

Mainly, though, God has shown me that "to whom much is given, much is required."

Being active in *Lady Finelle* is now only a part of the impossible dream. God stirred me with an excitement for the business world again because He knew He could trust me—that I wouldn't make it top priority again. Instead, He has given me a higher purpose—an even greater dream than any that I have had before!

Chapter Twenty-Two

The Most Possible, Impossible Dream of All

Back in 1977 when God first spoke to me about singing for Him, I really questioned it. The first indication I had that it *really* might work was when my friend, Ray, showed me those musical soundtracks in his home.

I felt I had really lost whatever musical talents I had that won me so much fame as Miss West Virginia years before. But I decided to give it a try as the Lord led. I went ahead and made the first step by contacting a vocal instructor for lessons. It seemed so futile; I had even lost my sense of rhythm.

Then, one day, Bill went out on his own and bought me a tape recorder and some sound equipment. It was his way of saying that his support and love were behind me. It was a great uplifting, but there was a lot of work ahead.

No matter how much of my former talent God restored, and no matter how much I practiced, it still seemed ridiculous for me to think about going out to sing—I knew it; my family knew it. But I also "knew that I knew that I knew" that God had most definitely called me into His service as a witness to sing for Him. He was obviously asking me to do the ridiculous so that He could do the miraculous.

I wish I could say that everything turned out fine from the start. Unfortunately, my first public attempts to sing were disasters. I made mistakes. I stumbled. It was so humiliating when I would mess up or get the words mixed up.

One time after singing in a little church in the mountains, I asked God, "Why? Why do I have to keep on doing this when I keep making mistakes? Why do I have to be so embarrassed?"

Instantly, the answer came back, "Because I am teaching you, and I am letting you make your mistakes in front of twenty people instead of the multitudes who will hear you in coming days."

I thanked Him for His compassion, but it still hurt so bad as I continued plodding on. The old self took a beating; I was broken into little pieces so God could mold me back together like He wanted to.

Two years after I first felt the call to begin singing again (and after a number of singing engagements, I had finally started to get a little confidence back in my musical abilities), God added another blockbuster.

Had He revealed His total plan back in 1977, I probably would have backed off completely, but I heard Him call me into music, so I took the initial steps, and God blessed my efforts.

Then, in 1979, we were at a Full Gospel Businessmens' meeting, and God showed me that I would not only be *singing* for Him, but from that point on I would be *speaking* and giving my testimony.

I had known from the beginning that He was going to do a fast work within me, but I never had any idea that it would happen as fast as that.

That evening at the Full Gospel Businessmen's meeting, the Spirit of the Lord came over me, and I began weeping as I listened to the speaker. After weeping all evening—knowing God was about to begin something unknown and unusual—I arrived home and felt compelled to go into the living room and open my Bible. God seemed to have a special message for me, and I knew that this was an ordained appointment with God.

Opening the Bible, my eyes immediately fell on the passage of Scripture where Paul was giving his testimony of Jesus' calling on his life to King Agrippa. The words were emblazoned on my heart:

"Now stand up! For I have appeared to you to appoint you as my servant and witness. You are to tell the world about this experience and about the many other occasions when I shall appear to you. And I will protect you from both your own people and the Gentiles. Yes, I am going to send you to the Gentiles to open their eyes to their true condition so that they may repent and live in the light of God instead of Satan's darkness, so that they may receive

186

forgiveness for their sins and God's inheritance along with all people everywhere whose sins are cleansed away, who are set apart by faith in me" (Acts 26:1-18, *The Living Bible*).

I read the verses again and again. The Spirit of God had been upon me all evening, and I felt humbled to see His work growing within me.

It sounded ridiculous for me to go out speaking, even more ridiculous than just singing, but I received His Word as the light for my path.

I also asked God for a confirmation. He provided *two* of them to assure me that I was following His path.

The following Monday morning, I received a letter from Gloria, a friend of my sister, Joyce, in Ohio—she had a word for Les and me, that we would be moving into a far-reaching ministry. Les had already gone to PTL's Heritage School of Evangelism and Communication, so his ministry was expanding all the time. (Les is also employed with PTL as a cable-satellite marketing representative.)

The very next Full Gospel Businessmen's meeting, Larry Allen, a well-known speaker (then an employee with the PTL Television Network in Charlotte), was ministering. He startled me by asking everyone to turn to Acts 26: 1-18; he began reading Paul's testimony to King Agrippa.

After his message, Larry prayed, then looked up at me and pointed. He said, "Stand up!"

"Me?" I asked.

"You," he replied. "I have a message for you."

He proceeded to ask me to come down to the front of the building. He asked the people there to stretch their hands toward me, then began prophesying—giving me the exact confirmation that I had asked for after the previous Full Gospel meeting!

Only God could do something that good and complete. The Holy Spirit is such a perfect Guide.

From that point, the roller-coaster ride took off in high gear. Suddenly, I began getting requests to speak at churches, Women's Aglow meetings, conferences, youth rallies. I became the president of my local Aglow chapter. My story and full-color picture were even featured in the Aglow Magazine, a periodical that goes all over the world.

I have continued to give my testimony on a number of radio and television programs—even the very Christian talk show that changed my life so dramatically by introducing me to the Holy Spirit. So many doors for ministry are opening now. I still stand amazed in His presence at what He is able to do.

God has shown us that he is leading my family into His ministry, too. Les and Becky have already traveled with me on several occasions. There have been teaching seminars where I have done the teaching, while Les and Becky have each ministered in song.

The most important thing of all that God has shown me through these past months is that everything I have gone through has happened specifically to bring me to this, the most exciting time in my life. All that I've learned, all that I've experienced can now be told so that others may find Christ as their own personal Savior. I know that if He can do it for me, He can make it work for anybody.

Just months ago, I had a dream—a panoramic vision from God as vivid and colorful as anything on a Hollywood screen. In it, I was standing on the deck of our home, gazing at the breath-taking view of the mountains. In this dream, I stood looking up at the sky, and I saw a man's face appear. He seemed to be in his early thirties, but he had unusually thick glasses on. I was puzzled, but as I continued looking at the sky, another face appeared alongside the first man's, then another, then another. One-by-one the faces appeared until the entire sky was filled with faces.

Then, the dream ended.

When I woke up, I knew that I had been in the presence of God. I was in a spirit of worship and praise, and I knew that God was showing me the next step in my life. I just didn't know how the pieces of the puzzle fit together or what the dream meant.

I even asked the Lord, but I received no immediate answer, so I got up, fixed breakfast for Bill and the children, then went in to get ready for the day's activities.

Suddenly, the Lord spoke to me. "Do you know what that dream meant?"

I said, "No."

He spoke again: "These are the faces of the people you will bring into My Kingdom as a result of your testimony."

"But why the thick glasses on the first man's face?" I asked.

"The people are spiritually blind."

It reminded me of the Word He had shown me after that Full Gospel meeting, Paul's testimony from Acts 26:18, "to open their eyes to their true condition so that they may repent and live in the light of God instead of in Satan's darkness, so that they may receive forgiveness for their sins and God's inheritance along with all people everywhere whose sins are cleansed away, who are set apart by faith in Him."

What could I say? Why had God chosen me?

I had never known why I had to go through all that I'd experienced to get to this point. The first impossible dream that led me from a poverty-stricken childhood to the top of the business world nearly destroyed me and everything I had. Surely there could have been a more direct route than the one I took—one with less struggles and pitfalls. And why did the problems have to be compounded by the hypoglycemia that weakened my body so? Why did I have to get so low and go through so much before I saw the Light-giver?

Obviously, there are many people who have gone through (or are going through) similar experiences—people who need to know that there is a better way, that there *is* hope even in that deep, dark pit, that Christ *can* change unchangeable circumstances, and that the Holy Spirit *can* be the Giver of life and joy.

Slowly, the truth sank in as I thought about the vision. Each impossible dream had just been a stepping stone to the next dream.

Now, I was challenged with the greatest dream of all—the one of countless faces waiting to hear the Good News that Jesus Christ loves them and died for them.

I've been told that every three seconds that pass, another person dies somewhere in the world; and that nine out of every ten people who do die may not know Jesus as their personal Savior.

That burdens me. I cannot help but think about the people who need to hear the life-giving Gospel. Those people are the faces in my vision—waiting to hear.

So, it is time to move on. I have faced challenges before, but now I am faced with what seems to be the most impossible dream of all.

I'm one woman with a near-tragic story, but in Jesus I am so much more. I am more than the successful business woman that people see recognized at cosmetic conventions, and I am more than the woman who sings and speaks at services, meetings, and on TV.

I am the woman who almost never made it at all. And I know from personal experience what Jesus was talking about in Matthew 19:26, "With men this is impossible; but with God all things are possible."

I've seen so many impossible dreams become possible. And I want to tell the world of the impossible dreams that can come true for them.

As for me, I know that the *real* dream is just beginning.